AND SO IT IS!

AND SO IT IS!

A Repository of Memories

SHORT STORIES

POEMS

SERMONS

NARRATIVES

ALBERT F. SCHMID

iUniverse, Inc.
Bloomington

And So It Is!
A Repository of Memories

iUniverse books may be ordered through booksellers or by contacting:

iUniverse
1663 Liberty Drive
Bloomington, IN 47403
www.iuniverse.com
1-800-Authors (1-800-288-4677)

ISBN: 978-1-4502-9306-8 (sc)
ISBN: 978-1-4502-9308-2 (hc)
ISBN: 978-1-4502-9307-5 (ebk)

Printed in the United States of America

iUniverse rev. date: 05/22/2012

CONTENTS

PREFACE

Disclaimers and Dedications

It has always been my desire to write a book about something or another. You know the old saying about good intentions. I cannot claim that I have authored each story in this manuscript, but as the stories developed they were used to illustrate the theme of each devotional that I gave. It became apparent that it would be interesting to put them together in a book. And so it is.

I appreciate the opportunity to join with the members of the Outreach and Visitation Committees at the First Baptist Churches of East Greenwich and Wickford, RI who invited me to share the Good News with folks in the local nursing homes. It has inspired me to write other short stories and articles, but most with a religious connotation.

Someone once asked me where I got my stories. Did they happen or did I make them up?

The answer is that they come from many sources. My sister Jane Charles often sends me tidbits that have beautiful spiritual illustrations and I weave them into the sermons. Other stories are from memories of my family. Many are inspired by the scripture verses themselves.

My wife Audrey is my number one critic and auditor. Her encouragement and direction has been positive.

One thing that has motivated me to develop my writing and preaching skills is this admonition:

> **"Accomplish more than we thought we could,**
> **Be more than we were before,**
> **And count the many blessings that God has provided."**

> "We are . . . Christ's ambassadors, as though God were making
> his appeal through us."
> 2 Corinthians 5:20

BLESSINGS

A Blessing cannot be kept. If it is stopped with the recipient, then the blessing disappears.

We are blessed significantly in many ways, but particularly by being a member of the First Baptist Church East Greenwich, RI. The church provides us with the opportunity to minister and evangelize while serving on the Visitation Committee and as Pastor of Elder-Care.

We are the recipients of a blessing and we need to keep that blessing working by being the source of the blessing to other people.

Rev. Albert F. Schmid

A PRAYER TO
CHANGE YOUR LIFE

Sometime around three thousand years ago, one of history's great nobodies decided to pray. When he looked at himself and his circumstances, he saw no reason for hope. But when he prayed, he prayed the boldest and most hopeful prayer he could imagine. And God answered him.

God is still answering. The prayer, of a man named *Jabez,* is motivating millions of people today to seek the Lord in a new way, to cry out to Him for blessings, and to reach for a larger and more full filling life in HIS service.

Too many people put off doing something that brings them joy because they haven't thought about it, or don't have it on their schedule, or didn't know it was coming or didn't think it was possible.

Someone once said there is really very little difference between people—but that *little difference*—makes all of the difference in the World.

If you haven't read *THE PRAYER OF JABEZ,* I highly recommend that you do. If you are new to the story, you'll find it in *1 Chronicles,* buried in the official genealogies of the tribes of Israel. The historian, writing about 500 years B.C. traces the official family tree of the Jews from Adam through thousands of years up to his own time. The first nine chapters of the book are taken up with naming the names, hundreds of them—most of them unfamiliar and hard to pronounce. It is the most boring book in the Bible

Suddenly in the Fourth Chapter . . . . one name, the forty-fourth, deserves special comment: *"Now Jabez was more honorable than his brothers, and his mother called his name Jabez, saying, "Because I bore him in pain." And Jabez called on the God of Israel saying, "Oh, that YOU would bless me indeed, and enlarge my territory, that YOUR hand would be with me, and that YOU would keep me from evil, that I may not cause pain." So God granted him what he requested.*

1 Chronicles 4: 9-10

1

In the next verse, the roll call continues as if nothing has happened—*Chelub, Shuah, Mehir . . . .* You can scour from front to back in the Bible looking for more insight into this man *Jabez*, and you will find nothing. A simple man made a simple prayer to God and God granted him what he requested.

In Hebrew the name *Jabez* means pain. A literal rendering could read, "He causes (or will cause) pain." All babies arrive with a certain amount of pain, but *Jabez's* birth went beyond the usual. His mother could not understand it.

We know simply that things started badly for a person no one had heard of: he prayed an unusual one sentence prayer; and things ended extraordinarily well.

Jabez's prayer asked for four things: (1) He asked God to Bless him. (2) He asked God to enlarge his territory, (3) He asked God to be with him . . . . and (4) He asked God to keep him from evil so that he would not cause anyone else to have pain.

That one prayer and a life that was more honorable than his brothers, earned *Jabez* a place of honor in Israel's history books. Fortunately for us, his mini-biography reveals an intriguing record of personal transformation.

If we look hard enough, we will find hiding behind each of *Jabez's* request a truth that can change our lives and our futures.

Personal change begins when you cry out to God . . . . *for what He wants for you*—with hands open and heart expectant. Miracles begin here. Each day you'll see new beginnings and new opportunities. You will think new thoughts. The direction of your life will shift, and your name like *Jabez's* will be headed for God's honor roll for all of eternity.

Dear Lord, thank you for making me in your image.
And preparing me for a wonderful and important destiny.
Forgive me for withdrawing into my own meager and limiting dreams.
When I do this, I deny you the freedom to use me as your mouth,
Hands, and heart.
I want to fulfill your world-sized dream for me every day of my life In
Eternity, I want to run into your arms hearing the words, "Well done."
Please expand my influence and impact for you beyond all that
I can imagine. I am your devoted servant. Here am I Lord . . . send me.

FIVE FINGER PRAYER

1. Your thumb is nearest you. So begin your praying with it. Pray for those closest to you. They are the easiest to remember.
2. The next finger is the pointing finger. Pray for those who teach, instruct and heal. Includes teachers, doctors and Ministers. They need support in pointing others in the right direction.
3. The next finger is the tallest finger. It reminds us of our Leaders. Pray for the president, the leaders of our country and the leaders of business and industry. For our newly elected officials.
4. The fourth finger is our ring finger. Surprising to many this is the weakest finger, as any piano teach will tell us. It reminds us to pray for those who are weak, in trouble and in pain.
5. And lastly, comes our little finger, our pinky, the smallest finger which is where we should place ourselves in relation to God and others. The Bible says, "The least shall be the greatest among you." Our little finger should remind us to pray for ourselves. By the time we have prayed for the other four groups our own needs will be put in proper perspective and we will be able to pray for yourself more effectively.

THE OLD MAN'S HANDS

Scripture: Psalm 63: 1-5

O God, you are my God,
Earnestly I seek you.
My soul thirsts for you,
In a dry and weary land,
Where there is no water.

I have seen you in the sanctuary
And beheld your power and your glory.
Because your love is better than life.
My lips will glorify you, I will praise you.
As long as I live, and in your name
I *will lift up my hands.*
My soul will be satisfied as with the richest of foods,
With singing lips my mouth will praise you.
Amen

David describes his feelings about his relationship with God. He says that he "*Earnestly seeks HIM.*" His soul thirsts for Him. He says that he has "Seen God in the sanctuary" and has beheld His Power and Glory. David proclaims that "GOD'S LOVE IS BETTER THAN LIFE."

And he declares that his lips will glorify Him, he will praise Him as long as he lives.

David promises that he will lift up his HANDS. Lifting ones' hands is an act of praise or acclamation and David gives God an enthusiastic vote of approval. He "Lifts" his hands in PRAISE.

When was the last time that you really looked at your hands? I mean really looked at your hands.

Once a young man watched an elderly man, who was probably 90 years old, sitting quietly on a park bench. The old man didn't move just sat with his head down, staring at his hands.

The young man sat down next to the old man, he didn't acknowledge his presence. He wondered if the old man was okay

Finally, the young man not really wanting to disturb him, but wanting to check on him, asked, "Are you okay?" The old man raised his head and looked, and smiled.

Yes, I am fine, thank you for asking he said in a clear strong voice.

I didn't mean to disturb you sir, but you were sitting here staring at your hands and I wanted to make sure that you were Okay, said the young man.

"HAVE YOU EVER LOOKED AT YOUR HANDS?" He asked. Well, No, I guess that I have never really looked at my hands, he answered, wondering what was his point.

The old man smiled and related this story:

1. Stop and think for a moment about the hands that you have. How they served you well throughout the years. These hands, though wrinkled, shriveled and weak have been the tools that I have used all my life to reach out and grab and embrace life.
2. They put food in my mouth. Clothes on my back.
3. As a child my mother taught me to fold them in prayer.
4. They caressed the love of my life.
5. They held my rifle and wiped my tears when I went off to war.
6. They have been dirty.
7. They have been scraped and raw, swollen and bent.
8. They were uneasy and clumsy when I tried to hold my newborn son.
9. Decorated with my wedding band they showed the World that I was married.
10. They wrote the letters home.
11. They shook and trembled when I buried my parents and my spouse.
12. They perspired when I walked my daughter down the aisle

13. And yet they were strong and sure when I dug my buddy out of the foxhole.
14. And when I lifted the plow off of my best friend's foot.
15. They have held children, consoled neighbors, and shook a fist in anger.
16. They covered my face, combed my hair and cleansed the rest of my body.
17. They have been sticky and wet, bent and broken, dried and raw.
18. Even now . . . . when not much of anything else on my body works well,
19. These hands hold me up, lay me down and continue to fold in prayer.
20. It will be these hands that God will reach out and take when he leads me home.
21. He won't care about where these hands have been or what they have done.
22. What God will care about is to whom these hands belong and how much He Loves me.
23. He will care about whom these hands belong to.
24. With these hands He will lift me to His side and there I will use these hands to TOUCH the face of Christ.

The young man left the park. He never saw the old man again, but he said that he would never forget him and the words that he spoke. And he said that when his hands hurt, or are sore, or when he strokes the face of this children and touches his wife he thinks of the Old man in the park.

I believe that old man has been stroked and caressed and held by the hands of God, and I too want to touch the face of God and feel his hands upon my face.

Thank you, Father God, for hands. AMEN.

Close with prayer.

THE CHRISTMAS TRADITION

I was listening to a radio commentator last night who reminded me that there are only 22 days left before Christmas. Whew! Where has the time gone? Seems like it was just yesterday that we were enjoying Halloween and Thanksgiving holidays. Here it is December and we are rocketing toward Christmas at Mach 4 speed. Only 22 days to go.

As I pondered about what I wanted to talk to you about today, I thought we needed to reflect on this time of year and the events leading up to the 25th of December. What is Christmas?

I turned to my Bible and its concordance and looked up the word CHRISTMAS. It wasn't there. I quickly went to my Bible Dictionary and found the definition. Christmas is the anniversary of the birth of Jesus Christ and its observance is celebrated by most Protestants and Catholics on the 25th of December. Eastern Orthodox churches celebrate Christmas on January 6 and Armenian Churches on January 19.

The first mention of Christmas on December 25th is in the time of Constantine, about 325 A.D. The actual date of Jesus' birth is unknown.

The word CHRISTMAS is formed by **Christ + Mass,** meaning a mass of religious service in commemoration of Jesus' birth. And so we find ourselves preparing for the celebration of the birth of God's son.

The Christian Church has a period called Advent which leads up to Christmas. It is a time that is rich with traditions and symbols. Many of these had their origins in pagan traditions. But Christians interpreted many of them in spiritual ways to help themselves as well as new believers to focus on Christ.

Advent is four weeks of lighting candles, counting the days, waiting with hopeful hearts for the arrival of that **SACRED DAY.**

THE ADVENT WREATH is a very popular tradition. It traces its origin back to pre-Christian Germany and Scandinavia, where the people gathered to celebrate the return of the Sun after the winter solstice. The circular wreath made of evergreens, with candles interspersed, represented the circle of the year and the life that endures through the winter months.

As the days grew longer people lit candles to offer thanks to the "Sun God" for added light. It started as a pagan tradition.

Lutherans in Eastern Germany are the ones who started the Advent wreath as a Christian religious custom. Today we celebrate Advent with the wreath and the progressive lighting of candles. The first candle lit is the **HOPE Candle.**

The HOPE candle is usually purple in color.

The second candle is the **BETHLEHEM** candle, symbolizing the Christ child's cradle. This candle is called the **LOVE** candle and is usually blue in color.

The third candle is the **SHEPHERD'S** candle and is either pink or rose. This candle typifies the act of sharing Christ. The candle is also known as the **JOY** candle.

The fourth candle is the **ANGEL'S** candle. It is the candle of love and the final coming. It is also known as the **PEACE** candle. It is usually colored red.

The largest candle, colored white, is placed in the center of the wreath. It is the **CHRIST candle** and it is traditionally lit on Christmas Eve.

CHRISTMAS TREES are another familiar symbol of Christmas. At this time of year the leaves of other types of trees have turned color and brown and have fallen from the tree. The evergreen tree keeps its fresh green look and is adorned with ornaments and lights symbolizing **LIFE.**

By the beginning of the 19th century all of Germany had adopted the use of the green fir tree known as the **Christmas tree.** The tree was decorated with candles, stars, sweetmeats, tiny toys and gilded nuts.

The custom of the Christmas Tree was brought to the United State by the Pennsylvania Germans in the 1820's. In 1923 President Calvin Coolidge held the first lighting of an outdoor Christmas tree at the White House. It started a long standing tradition that has lasted to this day.

The White House tree is a giant spruce that stands over 50 feet in height and is decorated with more than 15,000 lights.

In lighting Christmas candles and/or lights we are reminded that Jesus is the light of the world . . . . the light that we should follow. Scripture reminds us that Jesus said:

> *"I am the light for the world. Follow me and you won't be walking in the dark.*
> *You will have the light that gives life." John 8:12.*

There are many more traditions and symbols that remind us of the birth of Jesus. They include:

The Advent Calendar, the bells, the Candles, even candy canes. Christmas carols, cards and letters. Christmas Eve services. Manger scenes, mistletoe, poinsettia plants, ivy, Yule logs and more.

You can reflect on your memories of Christmas past. Good memories I trust. For those of us who sincerely wish to observe the season properly we need to slow down and put Christ back into our lives and remember that Jesus brings light into darkness. He is the truth and the light of the way.

I WISH EACH AND EVERYONE A MERRY CHRISTMAS. GOD BLESS YOU.

As Old As I Used To Be

The grocery store is a great place to get food for your body, but I discovered recently that it is a better place to find nourishment for your heart, mind and soul. This happened the other day as I was walking through a super market to pick up a quart of milk. You know how the dairy section is always located at the opposite end of the building.

As I walked toward the dairy section I heard two ladies standing by the fruit counter catching up on old times. The first lady jokingly asked her friend how old she was. The second lady replied in a loud voice, "Honey I'm not nearly as old as I used to be." Everyone within earshot laughed.

But as I was leaving the checkout counter I realized that I am not nearly as old as I used to be either. I am not as old as I was when I constantly worried about my bills and how I was going to pay them. Or how I was going to cope with a problem that was nagging me. Or what should I expect to happen to me tomorrow. Now I just trust in God and I always seemingly have a solution. God provides me with my needs.

I'm not as old as I used to be when I worried about my weight and my thinning grey hair.

Now I just look in the mirror and smile. The body looks older but the soul on the inside is younger than ever.

I'm not as old as I used to be when I was judging others, getting angry with them or worrying about what they thought of me. Now I do my best to judge no one. I try to love everybody and share my joy with the world. Life is too short to live any other way.

You don't have to be as old as you used to be either. God made all of us ageless and forever young by choosing love, joy and oneness with Him, through His son Jesus Christ. You can always keep growing younger on the inside by sharing these truths with others. In sharing the love and joy that you receive with others around the world. By living from your soul you can stop counting your chronology and your birthdays and you can start living for eternity because you will never again be as old as you used to be.

> Scripture: *"In the Lord's hands is the life of every creature and the breath of all mankind. Does not the ear test words a the tounge tastes food? Is not wisdom found among the aged? Does not life bring understanding? To God belongs wisdom and power; counsel and understanding are his."* Job *12: 10-13*

Prayer

CHRISTMAS EVE

**The word CHRISTMAS was formed with two words, CHRIST +
MASS, meaning a mass of religious service in commemoration of the
birth of God's son. The first mention of CHRISTMAS observance on
December 25th began in the time of Constantine about 325 A.D.**

**And, we could go on and on talking about all of the wonderful
and beautiful things that help us to celebrate the birth of Jesus. We are
in fact acknowledging that Christ is with us.**

**I would like to take a minute and tell you a story about a little boy
who's unselfish act demonstrated that God is here and among us.**

This special little boy wanted to meet God. He knew it was a long
trip to where God lived so he decided to pack a lunch. He put in a bag of
potato chips and a six pack of Coca Cola and started his journey.

When he had gone about three blocks he met an old woman who was
sitting on a bench in the park, staring at some pigeons.

The boy sat down next to her and opened his lunch. He was about
to take a drink of Coke when he noticed that the old lady looked hungry,
so he offered her some of his chips. She smiled and gratefully accepted
some.

Her smile was pretty and the boy wanted to see it again. So he offered
her a Coke. She smiled and took it. They sat there all afternoon eating and
smiling, but they never said a word.

As the twilight approached the boy realized how tired he was and he
got up to leave, but before he had gone more than a few steps, he turned
and ran back to the old woman and gave her a big hug. She gave him her
biggest smile.

When the little boy returned home, his mother was surprised by the
look of joy on his face. She asked him "What did you do today that made
you so happy?" He replied, "I had lunch with God." But before his mother
could respond, he added.

"You know what? She's got the most beautiful smile I have ever seen."

Meanwhile, the old woman, also radiant with joy, returned to her home. Her son was surprised by the look of peace on her face and he asked "Mom, what did you do today that made you so happy?" She replied, "I ate potato chips in the park with God." But before her son could comment, she added, "You know, he is much younger than I expected

Too often we under estimate the power of a touch, a radiance of a smile, or the sound of a kind word, a listening ear, an honest compliment, or the smallest act of caring.

Each of us has the potential to make it a **Christmas Day,** any day, for those who come into our lives.

> Romans 8:28 "And we know that in all things God works
> For the good of those who love Him, who
> Have been called according to His purpose."

Because this is Christmas Eve, we should end our service by remembering the legend of the candy cane. The candy cane is a symbol of the humble roots of Christianity. The shepherd's crook. In 1670 the choir-master at the Cologne Cathedral in Massachusetts handed plain white sugar sticks to his young singers to keep them quiet during the long ceremony. In honor of the occasion he had the sticks bent into shepherds' crooks.

The hardness of the candy cane reminds us that the church was founded on a solid rock.

The traditional peppermint flavor tastes like hyssop, a plant in the mint family. It was used in the old Testament for purification and sacrifice.

In 1920 the candy cane became more recognizable when striping was added. We are reminded of Christ's blood and His purity by the red and white stripes. The wider red stripes remind us of the blood that Jesus shed on the cross. The smaller red stripes symbolize the stripes and wounds that he received. The white stripes represent Christ's sinless purity.

And if we happen to forget all of this, we simply turn the cane over and it becomes the letter "J" which reminds us of Jesus our Lord.

Prayer

A Super Sunday

A lot of people have been waiting many weeks and months for Sunday. For them it is a **special day.** It is Super Sunday. Some of you know what I'm talking about. Certainly most of the men and boys in the country know what this is all about. This is the big day for **professional football.** It has been a long, tough season, and even though you may or not be a football fan you can't help but listen to the hype on radio and TV, read about the players, the coaches, and the teams in the newspaper, and wonder if the whole country hasn't gone a little daffy over a ball made out of pig skin.

Super Bowl Sunday is almost here. The **New England Patriots** are playing the **Philadelphia Eagles** in Jacksonville, Florida this Sunday. **The Patriots** are the defending Super Bowl Champions and are trying to win the title again this year, for the third consecutive time. Isn't that exciting?

Sunday these two teams will play the best they can, each hoping that it will be good enough to win. Not only is winning quite an honor, but the players earn a lot of money if they win—or even if they don't win. In order to be able to play in the **Super Bowl**, the members of these two teams had to work hard in practice, listening carefully to what the coaches told them to do. Then, all season long, from mid-August to mid-January, they put into practice what they have learned. In other words, they had to play hard and get better and better in order to win all of their games and get a chance to play in the **Super Bowl.**

You may not think of yourself as a football player. You may not even have a friend or acquaintance who is into football. You may not even like football. But, even so, Sunday can be a *Super Sunday* for you. In fact, each Sunday of the year can be a super Sunday. How can we make it so?

You are the team and I'll be the coach. I will tell you two ways to make each Sunday a *Super Sunday.* The first way is to work hard during the week. I want my team to work hard at being good to others every day of the week. When you help others play the game of life better, you find that you are winning the game of life yourself. If you want to feel super on Sunday, just try being good to others all week.

The second way to make every Sunday super. is to prepare yourself for Sunday so that you can really come to worship God, I've heard people say "I didn't get a thing out of Church today." Which has caused me to think, "**Well, maybe you didn't come prepared to get anything out of church.**" If you will worship God as you should—and, of course, this doesn't mean you are to worship God only on Sunday—you will prepare yourselves by **reading the Bible, by praying each day, and by listening for ways God speaks to your to tell you what you should do.**

So team, there are two things to do to make every Sunday a Super Sunday: give loving help to others during the week, and then prepare yourselves every day of the week to say to God, **"I love you."**

When we do this we will be doing what God wants us to do, and our Sundays will really be super.

A Story

A member of a church who had been attending services regularly suddenly stopped going to church. After a few weeks the pastor decided to visit him. When he arrived, the pastor found the man at home alone, sitting before a blazing fire.

The man welcomed the pastor in and invited him to sit in a comfortable chair near the fireplace. And he waited.

The pastor made himself at home, but said nothing. Silently, he watched the flames dance around the burning logs. After a few minutes the pastor took the fire tongs, carefully picked up a brightly burning ember and placed it to one side of the hearth. He then sat back and waited.

As the one lone ember's flames flickered and diminished, there was a momentary glow and then its fire was no more. **Soon it was cold and lifeless.**

The pastor glanced at his watch, realized it was time to leave, and he slowly stood up, quietly picked up the cold, dead ember and placed it back in the middle of the fire. It immediately began to glow once more with the light and warmth of the burning coals around it.

As the pastor reached the door to leave, the man said with a tear running down his cheek, **"Thank you so much for your visit and especially for the *fiery sermon*. I will be back in church next Sunday."**

We live in a world today which tries to say too much with too little. Consequently, few listen.

Sometimes the best sermons are the ones left unspoken.

"Let your light shine before men in such a way that they may see your good works and glorify your Father which is in heaven."
Matthew 5:16.

I hope and pray that **Sunday** will be a **Super Sunday** for you. God bless you.

WHAT IS GOOD ABOUT GOOD FRIDAY

There are three major holidays for Christians: **Christmas, Easter, and Pentecost.** You may have heard the old joke about **C & E Christians,** Christmas and Easter believers.

Christmas, is the anniversary of the birth of Christ and its observance is celebrated by Roman Catholics and Protestants, on December 25. The first mention of Christmas was made in the time of Constantine, about 325 AD. In spite of the world's effort to convert the holiday into a commercial event, we still focus on the true meaning of Christmas and celebrate the birth of Jesus, God's gift of His son to mankind.

Pentecost derives from the Greek, meaning the "fiftieth day". It was the Jewish Feast of Weeks, sometimes referred to as the Feast of Harvest, or the Day of the First-Fruits, which fell on the 50th day after the Feast of the Passover. In the book of Acts, Chapter 2, we learn of events that transformed the Jewish festival into a Christian one, making it a symbolic between it and the first fruits of the Christian dispensation. Pentecost is celebrated 50 days after Easter Sunday. Many believe that **Pentecost** is the establishing of the Christian Church

Easter is the day on which the Church celebrates the resurrection of Jesus Christ. In 325 AD the Council of Nices ruled that Easter should be celebrated on the first Sunday after the full moon following the eternal equinox. The date of Easter varies between the 22nd of March and the 25th of April.

Practicing Christians observe two additional holidays. **Ash Wednesday,** which occurs on the Wednesday before the first Sunday in Lent, or six weeks before Easter Sunday, and **Good Friday** which is the Friday before Easter.

Good Friday is a celebration of the passion, suffering and death by crucifixion of Jesus. Several years ago, when my youngest son was about six years of age, we were preparing to attend a **Good Friday** service at our church. He asked me a very interesting question. He said, **"Why do they call it Good Friday if that is the day that Jesus was killed"**

The day that Jesus died is called **Good Friday** because it was a good day for mankind. Jesus died for us, in our place, that we may have forgiveness of sin. The day was both a happy day and a sad day. It was sad day because Jesus suffered and died on the cross, but it was a happy day because Jesus paid the penalty for our sins. At the time the day was not seen as good, but Easter morning after Jesus arose from the dead everyone knew it was good. Because of the passion of Christ, the result is salvation for sinners and therefore the day is called *Good.*

The liturgy reflects on **Love** as much as it does on **Loss. Worshipers** reflect not only on their own sinfulness but also on God's incomparable **Love** for us.

> John 19: 17-18 says,
> *"He was taken out of the city, he carried his cross by himself. He went out to a place known as the "The Skull",*
> *in Hebrew is was called Golgotha.*
> *There they crucified him and two others with him.*
> *One was on either side, with Jesus between them.".*

Crucifixion was a horrible event. The agony of the crucified victim was brought about by a number of factors.

(1) The painful character of the wounds inflicted by nailing of the victim to the cross.

(2) The suffering caused by the abnormal position of the body, arms outstretched with the weight pulling down.

(3) The traumatic fever induced by hanging for a long period of time.

Blood sinks rapidly into the lower extremities of the body and within 6 to 12 minutes blood pressure drops to less than 50%. The heart is deprived of blood which ultimately results in heart failure. Death by crucifixion did not generally happen for two to three days. Death was often hasten by breaking the victims legs which induced further shock and trauma. With Jesus, the soldiers saw that he was already dead so they did not break his legs (John 19:33)

PICTURE THE CROSS
This fulfilled prophecy.
I know a story too dear to hear
It comes in the form of a cross.
It's tale that has lasted two thousand years.
It cannot be hidden or lost.

The sight of the Cross, all on its own
Requires no words to make clear.
Its image is old and very well known
Yet each time it is seen it brings tears.

It's a picture of shame, or grief and of pain,
A tale of the blood of the lamb.
There's no need for words, its vision explains
Quite plainly God's plan for man.
The Cross speaks volumes without making a sound,
We need only to see where its pierced.
And look on the ground for a dropped thorny crown,
To know of suffering and anguish most fierce

I cringe from the sound of silent screams heard,
Some of them coming from me.
For that sight of the cross without and words,
Is almost too deafen to see

"For God so loved the world that he gave his only begotten Son, that whosoever believes in Him should not perish but have everlasting life."
John 3:16

WHAT IS THE PRICE

How often do we learn of a story that clearly and succinctly tells us what we need to know?

Maybe not often enough. This Story provides a very clear lesson. This is one of those stories.

Once there was a man named George Thomas, a pastor, in a small New England town. One Sunday morning he came to church carrying a rusty. bent, old bird cage and sat it on the pulpit. The members of the congregation wondered what he was going to say.

Eyebrows were raised, and as if in response, the Pastor Thomas began to speak . . . He said. "I was walking through town yesterday when I saw a young boy coming towards me swinging this bird cage. On the bottom of the cage were three little wild birds, shivering with cold and frightened almost to death. I stopped the lad and asked, "What have you got in the cage son?" **"Just some old birds,"** came the reply.

"What are you going to do with them?" asked the pastor. "Take 'em home and have fun with 'em," the boy answered. "I'm gonna **tease 'em** and **pull out their feathers,** and make 'em fight. I'm gonna have a real good time." "But you'll get tired of those birds sooner or later. Then what will you do?" asked the preacher.

Oh, I got some cats. said the boy. They like birds. I'll just give 'em to them.

The pastor was silent for a moment and then said, "How much do you want for those birds, son?

Huh! You don't want them birds, mister. They are just plain old field birds. They don't sing, they don't do anything, they ain't even pretty. The pastor asked again, "How much?" The boy sized up the pastor as if he were crazy, and said, "$10.00."

The pastor reached into his pocket and took out a ten dollar bill. He placed it in the boy's hand and in a flash the boy was gone.

The pastor gently carried the cage to the alley where there was a tree, put the cage down, opened the door and coaxed the little birds to come out. He placed them in the tree setting them free.

That explained the empty cage that was on the pulpit. But the pastor began to tell the rest of the story.

He said:

"One day Satan and Jesus were having a conversation. Satan had just come from the Garden of Eden and he was gloating and boasting "Yes sir, I just caught me a world full of people down there. I set a trap, used bait they couldn't resist. I call it **SIN**. Got them all, every one of them."

"What are you going to do with them?" asked Jesus. "Oh, I'm gonna have fun with them," Satan replied. "I'm going to teach them to marry and divorce each other, how to hate and abuse each other, how to lie and cheat on each other, how to drink and smoke and curse. I'm gonna teach them how to invent **guns** and **bombs** and how to kill each other. I'm really gonna have fun."

"And what will you do when you get done with them?" Jesus asked. "Oh, I'll kill them and let them **burn in Hell**," Satan glared proudly.

"How much do you want for them?" Jesus asked.

"Oh, you don't want those people. They ain't no good. If you take them they will hate you. They will spit you, curse you and crucify you. You don't want those people."

How much? Jesus asked.

Satan looked at Jesus and sneered, **"All your blood, your tears and your life!"**

Jesus smiled and said, "DONE." And he paid the price.

The pastor picked up the cage, opened the door and walked out of the church.

Prayer

GOING TO CHURCH

As I thought about what I would like to share with you today, I was reminded of the story about the minister who died and was waiting in the line at the Pearly Gates. Ahead of him was a fellow dressed in a loud shirt, leather jacket and jeans.

Saint Peter addressed the "cool guy." Who are you? said Saint Peter. "I need to know whether to admit you to the Kingdom of Heaven." The fellow answered, "I'm Peter Pilot, retired Delta Airlines Captain from Los Angles." Saint Peter checks his list, smiles and says to the pilot. "Take this silken robe and golden staff and enter into the Kingdom." The pilot goes into Heaven.

Next it is the Minister's turn. He stands erect and booms out, "I am Joseph Snow, Pastor of Saint Ann's in Pasadena for the last 43 years. Saint Peter consults his list. He says to the minister, "Take this cotton robe and wooden staff and enter into the Kingdom.

"Just a minute, says the Minister, "that man who was a pilot got a silken robe and golden staff, and I get cotton and wood. How can this be?"

"Up here we work by results", said Saint Peter, **"While you preached . . . people slept, while he flew . . . . people prayed."**

A lot of people approach going to church in about the same manner. My wife and I have talked about what we want from church but never completely agree. No single church has everything that we agree is necessary for spiritual growth. But, most Sundays we have found something about the church to carry us through times of disillusionment and doubt. Here's what I have learned:

1. **Faith** is not me and God **alone.** Being with a group of believers is what matters. They can be irritating, exasperating and occasionally cruel, but they teach me that to love others means loving and forgiving those who can be unlovable.
2. Though **Sermons** don't always inspire, they do connect us to the word and gives us a view that rises above the clamor that

we are drowning in. On a good Sunday a sermon re-adjusts my perspective and renews my hope.

3. **Hymns** allow me to give expression to buried emotions. The tunes direct my praise to the One who is the author of all that is. Without much outward expressions I can easily become obsessed with myself.

4. **Prayers** remind me that life isn't only about me. A community of faith is made up of Individuals with joys, pains and desires that are unknown to others unless expressed. Petitions to God become opportunities for service and celebration.

5. I stay connected to church because it connects me with the One who loves me, and compels me to do the same for others. We go to church to worship our Lord, and to be spiritually fed. We serve the Lord by working together to do His will.

I know churches aren't perfect. Never have been and never will be. They get wrapped up in mundane matters, often overlook those who are hurting and fail to reach out to the most needy. And it can be, and often is, very frustrating.

Sometimes it takes the eyes and ears of faith to recognize the presence of God in a church.

> *"If I have the gift of prophecy and can fathom all mysteries, and all knowledge and if I have a faith that can move mountains, but have not love, I am nothing. If I give all I possess to the poor and surrender my body to the flames, but have not love, I gain nothing."*

> *1 Corinthians 13:2*

A priest, a minister and a guru sat discussing the best positions for prayer, while a telephone repairman worked nearby. :Kneeling is definitely the best way to pray" said the priest. "No" said the minister, "I get better results standing with my hands out stretched to heaven." "Your are both wrong" the guru said, ""The most effective prayer position is lying down on the floor". Finally, the repairman could not contain himself any longer,

"Hey fellas," He interrupted, the best praying I ever did was when I was hanging upside down from a telephone pole."

We can do all types of philosophizing, but the bottom line what we do to represent God in the way that we live our lives. Sometimes it is the simple, practical ways that are the most meaningful and have the most results.

Going to Church. Do it with enthusiasm and love of God and fellow men.

Amen

BE KIND TO ONE ANOTHER

When you read Ephesians 4: 32, Paul gives us some very sound advice, he says, **"Be kind and compassionate to one another, forgiving each other, just as Christ God forgave you."**

I am reminded of the story that was told about an elderly lady who walked into a small country church one Sunday morning. The **friendly usher** greeter her at the door and helped her up the flight of steps. "Where would you like to sit?" he asked politely. "The front row please" she answered. "Oh you really don't want to do that" the usher said. "The pastor is really boring and the sermon will be very dull." "Do you know who I am?" the woman inquired. "No" he said. "I'm the **Pastor's mother**" she replied. "Do you know who I am?" he asked, "No" she said. "Good" he answered.

Isn't it interesting that we are often given the opportunity to be of service or witness at the most unexpected times and under the most unusual circumstances. Perhaps you have been in a similar situation and found that what you did or what you said wasn't exactly what you wanted to do. Or maybe it turned out okay.

God is always exposing us to situations that test us. I like the story about the man who was driving home from work one evening when he noticed a car that was disabled on the side of the road. He pulled up in front of the car and noticed that the driver was an older lady. He got out of his car and approached the stalled car.

She was worried that no one had stopped to help for several hours, and was this stranger going to hurt her? He didn't look safe; he looked like he was poor and hungry.

He could see that she was frightened, and standing out there in the cold, he said, "I'm here to help you ma'am. Why don't you wait in my car where is its warm? By the way, my name is **Bryan Anderson.**"

Well, she had a flat tire. But, for an old lady that was bad enough. Bryan crawled under the car looking for a place to put the jack. He skinned his knuckles and got dirt on his clothes and on his hands. Finally he was able to change the tire and get the car down off the jack.

The lady began to talk with him. "I'm from St. Louis and was only passing though" she said. She couldn't thank him enough for coming to her aid. Bryan smiled and as he was closing the trunk she asked," **"How much do I owe you?"**

Bryan never thought twice about being paid. This was not a job to him. It was helping someone in need, and God knows there were plenty of times when people had given him a hand in the past. He told her that if she really wanted to pay him back the next time she saw someone who needed help she could give that person the assistance they needed, and Bryan added, **"And think of me."**

The lady thanked Bryan and she started her car and drove off. It had been a cold and depressing day but things were beginning to improve.

A few miles down the road the lady saw a small café. She went in to grab a bite to eat and take the chill off before making the last leg of her trip. The café was a dingy looking place. Outside there were two old gasoline pumps. Inside the place was old, but neat and clean. The scene was unfamiliar to her.

The waitress came over and brought a clean towel to wipe her hands and make her comfortable. The waitress had a sweet smile but she looked tired. She had been on her feet all day The older lady notice that she nearly eight months pregnant, but she never let the strain and aches change her attitude. The woman wondered how someone who had so little could be so considerate and giving to a stranger. **Then she remembered Bryan.**

After the lady had finished her meal she paid with a $100 dollar bill. The waitress quickly went to get change but the lady slipped out the door and was gone by the time she got back. Then she noticed written on the napkin "You don't owe me anything, I have been there too." "Somebody once helped me, the way I'm helping you. If you really want to pay me back, here is what you do: Don't let this chain of love end with you."

Under the napkin were four more $100 bills. Later that night when she crawled into bed she was thinking about the money and what the lady had written. How could the lady have known how much she and her husband needed the money? With baby due next month, things were going to be tough.

She knew how worried her husband was, and as he lay sleeping next to her, she gave him a soft kiss and whispered soft and low, "Everything's gonna be all right. I love you **Bryan Anderson."**

There is an old saying "What goes around comes around."

You Ask Why I Follow Jesus

You ask why I follow Jesus?
Why I love Him the way I do?
When the world's turned away from His teachings
And people who serve Him are few.

It's not the rewards I'm after
Or gifts that I hope to receive
It's the presence that calls for commitment.
It's the Spirit I trust and believe.
*   The Lord doesn't shelter His faithful*
Or spare them all suffering and pain.

Like everyone else I have burdens,
And walk through my share of the rain.
Yet He give me a plan and a purpose,
And that joy only Christians have known,
I never know what comes tomorrow
But I do know I'm never alone.

It's the love always there when you need it;
It's the words that redeem and inspire,
It's the longing to ever be with Him
That burns in my heart like a fire.
So you ask why I love my Lord Jesus?
Well, friends that's so easy to see,
But the one that fills me with wonder is
Why Jesus loves someone like me.

FLAG FOLDING CEREMONY

The Uniformed Services Code, Flag Folding Ceremony, is a dramatic and uplifting way to honor the USA's flag on special days like Memorial Day, or Veterans Day, retirement ceremonies and funerals.

"The flag-folding ceremony represents the same religious principles on which our country was originally founded. The portion of the flag denoting honor is the canton of blue containing the stars which represent the states of the union. The field of blue dresses from left to right and is inverted when draped as a pall on a casket of a veteran who served our country in uniform"

"At the ceremony of **Retreat** the flag is lowered slowly, folded in a triangle and kept under watch throughout the night as a tribute to our nation's honored dead. The next morning it is brought out and at the ceremony of **Reveille**, it is run aloft quickly as a symbol of our belief in the resurrection of the body."

The **first fold** of our flag is a symbol of life.

The **second fold** is the symbol of our belief in eternal life.

The **third fold** is made in honor and remembrance of the veteran departing our ranks who gave a portion of life for the defense of our country to attain peace throughout the world.

The **fourth fold** represents our weaker nature, for as American Citizens trusting in God. It is to Him we turn in times of peace as well as in times of War for His divine guidance.

The **fifth fold** is a tribute to our country for in the words of Stephen Decatur, "Our country in dealing with other countries, may she always be right: but it is still our country right or wrong."

The **sixth fold** is for where our hearts lie. It is with our hearts that we pledge allegiance to the flag of the United States of America, and to the republic for which it stands, one nation, under God, indivisible, with liberty and justice for all.

The **seventh fold** is the tribute to our Armed Forces, for it is through the Armed Forces that we protect our country and our flag against all her enemies, whether they are within or outside the boundaries of our republic.

The **eighth fold** is a tribute to the one who entered into the **Valley of the shadow of death,** that we might see the light of day, and to honor mothers for whom it flies on Mother's Day.

The **ninth fold** is a tribute to womanhood: for it has been through their faith, love, loyalty and devotion that the character of men and women who have made this country great have been molded.

The **tenth fold** is a tribute to father, for he too has given his sons and daughters for the defense of our country since they were first born.

The **eleventh fold**, in the eyes of a Hebrew citizen, represents the lower portion of the seal of King David and King Solomon, and glorifies, in their eyes, the God of Abraham, Isaac and Jacob.

The **twelfth fold,** in the eyes of a Christian citizen, represents an emblem of eternity and glorifies, in their eyes, God the Father, the Son, and the Holy Ghost.

When the flag is completely folded, the stars are uppermost, reminding us of our National motto, **"In God We Trust."**

After the flag is completely folded and tucked in, it takes on the appearance of a cocked hat, ever reminding us of the soldiers who served under George Washington, and the sailors and marines who served under Captain John Paul Jones, followed by their comrades and shipmates in the Armed Forces of the United States preserving for us the rights, privileges and freedom that we enjoy today.

Exchanging Fear For Faith

John Gibson, a popular anchor man for Fox News has written a book entitled **"The War on Christmas"**. You may have heard him on TV in interview explaining how he has been digging up evidence about the liberal activists, lawyers and politicians, educators and media people who are leading the war on Christmas. It is the secularization of America's favorite holiday, and the ever stronger push toward a neutered "holiday" season so that non-Christians won't be the least bit offended.

For instance, he reports that in Illinois, state government workers were forbidden to say the words, **"Merry Christmas" while** at work. In Rhode Island, local officials banned Christians from participating in a public project to decorate the lawn at City Hall. In New Jersey a school banned instrumental versions of traditional Christmas carols. Arizona school officials ruled it unconstitutional for a student to make any reference to the religious history of Christmas in a class project.

Even merchants like JC Penny Company and Wal-Mart have instructed their employees to use the phrase, **"Happy Holidays"** rather than **"Merry Christmas"**. Some justify using **"Happy Holidays"** as an alternate to **"Merry Christmas"** by saying it means **"Happy Holy Day"** which is suppose to be more inclusive of all faiths. Isn't it interesting that this year the Jewish New Year, **Hanukah,** falls on December 25, **Christmas.**

Millions of Americans are starting to fight back against the secularist forces and against officials who would rather surrender in fear than to be seen as politically incorrect. We need to exchange our Fears for Faith. Whether we doubt out loud or only to ourselves, we pay the price for a negative attitude of faith.

Zechariah, who was Elizabeth's husband and the father of John the Baptist, was an example of negative attitude of faith when he was told by an angel that he was going to have a son, and his name was to be John. Zechariah responded by asking the angel Gabriel, *"How can I be sure of this? I am an old man and my wife is well along in years"*. **Luke 1:18.** He doubted the word of the angel and paid the price by being unable to speak until his child was born.

We need to replace our fear with faith. Mary, the mother of Jesus was visited by the Angel Gabriel and we read of her confrontation in **Luke 1: 29-35.**

> *Vs. 29. "Mary was greatly troubled at his words and wondered what kind*
> *Of greeting this might be. But the angel said to her, "Do not be afraid Mary, you have found favor with God. You will be with child and give Birth to a son and you will give him the name of Jesus."*
>
> *He will be great and will be called the Son of the Most High. The Lord God will give Him the throne of his father David, and he will reign over*
> *The house of Jacob forever, his kingdom will never end.*
>
> *"How can this be, Mary asked the angel, since I am a virgin?" The angel answered. "The Holy Spirit will come upon you, and the Power of the Most High will overshadow you.*
> *So the holy one to be born will be called the Son of God. Vs. 38. Mary answered . . . . "May it be to me as you have said".*

Do you find that hard to believe? No one was more surprised by this miracle than was Mary.

And no one was more passive than she was. God did everything. Mary didn't volunteer to help.

All that she did was to offer no resistance. Instead, she said, *"Behold the bond-slave of the Lord, may it be done according to your word"* **Luke 1:38**

Unlike Mary, we tend to want to assist God . . . . assuming our part is as important as His.

Or we resist, thinking we are too bad, or too busy, or incapable of doing His will. We miss out on the reason we were placed on earth, **so that He can live through us.** We need to be **so full** of Christ that we can say, like Paul, *"It is no longer I who lives, but Christ lives in me." Gal. 2:20*

When we think negatively we open the door to Satan to make our doubts and fears come true.

We need to replace our fear with faith. When we exchange fear for faith, we open the door to God, who can make good things happen

We get upset when we are told that celebrating Christmas in any public way is a violation of church and state separation. That certainly is not what the founders of our country intended when they wrote, "Congress shall make no law respecting an establishment of religion or prohibiting the free exercise thereof." Let's replace these fears and exercise our faith.

Proclaim that Jesus is Lord

In deference to the legal activist I want to wish you **A MERRY CHRISTMAS!**

Lord, forgive me for living in my fears and doubts instead of believing you and trusting You. Help me to exchange my fear for faith today: In Jesus Name. Amen.

WHAT WILL MATTER

Ready or not, someday it will all come to an end.

There will be no more sunrises, no minutes, no hours or days.

All the things you have collected, whether treasured or forgotten, will pass to someone else.

Your wealth, fame and temporal power will shrivel to irrelevance.

It will not matter what you owned or what you were owed.

Your grudges, resentments, frustrations, and jealousies will finally disappear

So too, your hopes and ambitions, plans, and to-do-lists will expire.

The wins and losses that once seemed so important will fade away.

It won't matter where you came from, or on what side of the tracks you lived. It won't matter whether you were beautiful or brilliant.

Even your gender or skin color won't matter.

So what will matter? How will the value of your days be measured?

What is relevant is not what you brought, but what you built.

Not what you got, but what you gave.

What will matter is not your success but your significance. Not what you learned but what you taught.

What will matter is every act of integrity, compassion, courage or sacrifice that enriched, empowered or encouraged others to emulate your example.

What will matter is not your competence, but your character.

What will matter are not how many people you knew, but how many people will feel a lasting loss when your are gone.

What will matter is not your memories, but the memories that live in the hearts of those who loved you. What will matter is how long you will be remembered, by whom and for what.

Living a life that matters doesn't happen by accident. It's not a matter of circumstance but of choice.

"Nothing in all creation is hidden from God's sight. Everything is uncovered and laid bare before the eyes of him to whom we must give account." Hebrews 4:13

CHOOSE TO LIVE A LIFE THAT MATTERS

DON'T CRITICIZE, CONDEMN OR COMPLAIN

While working for Aero Commander Aircraft Company in Bethany, Oklahoma, in 1965, as Manager of Marketing Training, I had an opportunity to enroll in a Dale Carnegie Course. One of the things that I remember in how to *"Win Friends and Influence People"* was the phrase: **"Don't Criticize, Condemn or Complain."** I am certain there were many other rules, but this one stuck with me.

In the Bible, in Paul's letter to the church at Philippi, simply states: *"Do everything without complaining, or arguing, so that you may become blameless and pure, children of God . . ." Philippians 2:14.*

That is easy to **say** and even to **think** . . . . but difficult to enforce. Aren't we always looking to criticize the other guy, or to blame him or her for our troubles, or complain that they didn't let us know the what the outcome would be?

I am reminded of the story of the young woman who came into the kitchen where her father was reading the newspaper at the table. Sinking into the chair across from him, she began to flood the room with a stream of complaints. "Her college professors were too strict . . . . her boyfriend wasn't dependable . . . . her roommate was a slob, and she had no idea what God wanted her to do with her life.

Without a word, her father stood, walked to the sink and filled three pots with water. The young woman watched, confused, as her father put three pots on the stove and turned up the heat. As the pots came to a boil, he gathered items from the pantry and the refrigerator.

Into the first pot, he dropped a handful of carrots.
Into the second pot, he slide a raw egg.
Into the third pot, he sprinkled a handful of coffee grounds.

After a few moments, he crossed his arms and turned to his daughter and said, "Come here, honey, and tell me what you see."

His daughter rose and looked into the pots. "Okay", she said, staring at the food tumbling in the boiling water. "What's the point, Dad?"

Her father reached for a spoon and scooped out a few bits of carrots. "These were hard when I put them into the water," he said, "but now they are soft." "And the egg was soft when I put it in, but now it is hard-boiled." "But, what about the coffee that was in the third pot?" "It hasn't changed. said the daughter. "No, it hasn't. But it turned plain water into something fragrant and delicious." "Want a cup?"

Here is the powerful lesson in that simple illustration. "Are we like a carrot, hard and snappish until we go limp in the heat of **adversity**?" "Or are we more like an egg, which begins with a soft heart but hardens under testing? Outside we may look exactly the same, but something on the inside has toughened." Or perhaps we are more like the coffee, in the heat of a stressful situation, we color our surroundings with fragrance and flavor?"

The next time life turns up the heat ask yourself: "**Am I behaving like a carrot, an egg, or a measure of coffee?**"

"**To succeed with determination, you must resist the temptation to complain, and overcome the distress of discouragement.**"

Even Jesus felt the need for rest, and on several occasions when he was beleaguered by disappointment he simply took time to rest. But with each fresh sunrise he rose and reapplied himself to the task at hand

David, the psalmist knew about discouragement, doubt and misgivings. He wrote: "**When doubts filled my mind, your comfort gave me renewed hope and cheer." Psalm 94:19**

David knew that he could look to God for help.

When we find ourselves feeling stressed and doubtful, we need to go to a quiet place where we can meet with God and let him speak to us. Don't spend the time rattling off your complaints, or criticizing or condemning . . . . God already knows our grievances and discouragements Instead, sit in silence, lift your thoughts toward the Father and let Him speak to your heart. He will comfort and encourage you—**if you will simply take time to listen.**

Amen

QUIET SERMONS

Ecclesiastes is a book found in the Old Testament. Ecclesiastes is the record of all that human thinking and natural religion has ever been able to discover concerning the meaning and goal of life. **Therefore, is does not tell of God's arguments, and admonitions but of God's record of man's arguments.**

Ecclesiastes was written by Solomon and the book is dramatically autobiographical. It tells of Solomon's experience and reflections while he was **out of fellowship** with God. Solomon may have been wise, but he didn't follow his own wisdom. The problem that Solomon faced was how to find happiness and satisfaction apart from God. He tried everything but he could not get the answers.

The conclusion, Solomon tells us in Ecclesiastes, Chapter 12: verse 13 and 14:. *"Everything you were taught can be put into a few words:*

> *Respect and obey God!*
> *This is what life is all about.*
> *God will judge everything we do,*
> *Even what is done in secret,*
> *Whether good or bad."*

Solomon writes in Chapter 9:17 following: *"The quiet words of the wise are more to be heeded than the shouts of the ruler of fools."*

To illustrate this I would like to share with you the following true story:

There was a young man by the name of Bill. He had wild hair, wore T-shirts with holes in them. His jeans were ragged and torn and his white sneaker needed cleaning and washing.

This was his wardrobe for his entire four years of college.

Bill was a brilliant young man. Kind of profound but very, very bright. He became a Christian while attending college.

Across the street from the campus was a well-dressed, very conservative church. They wanted to develop a ministry for the college students but weren't sure how to go about it.

One day Bill decided to go to the church. He walked in with his dirty sneakers, ragged jeans and T-shirt and his wild hair. The service had already started so Bill started down the aisle looking for a seat.

The church was completely packed and he couldn't find a seat. By now, the people were beginning to get a bit uncomfortable, but no one said anything.

Bill got closer and closer to the front and realized there were no seats, so he just squats down on the carpet in front of the pulpit. Now people began to really get uptight and the tension in the air was thick. About this time a deacon who was in the back of the church began to slowly make his way toward Bill.

The deacon was in his 80's, silver-gray hair, wore a three piece suit. An example of a Godly man, very elegant, very dignified, very courtly. He walked with a cane . . . and as he started walking toward the boy, everyone is saying to themselves that you can't blame him for what he was going to do. How can you expect a man of his age and his background to understand some college kid sitting on the floor next to the pulpit?

Seemed like it took a long time for the man to reach the boy. The church was utterly silent except for the clicking of the old man's cane. All eyes were focused on him. The minister couldn't even preach the sermon until the deacon did what he had to do.

Now they see the elderly man drop his cane on the floor, With great difficulty he lowers himself and sat down next to Bill, **and worshiped with him so he wouldn't be alone.**

Everybody choked up with emotion.

When the minister gained control, he said, "**What I am about to preach, you will never remember. What you have just seen you will never forget.**" Remember be careful how you live . . . . you may be the only Bible some people will ever read.

"I ask the Lord to bless you
As I pray for you today.
To guide you and protect you
As you go along the way.
His love is always with you,
His promises are always true,
And when we give Him all our cares,
You know he will see us through."

Murray Hunt, a friend of the family, once admonished a church he was preaching at with these words, "LOVE GOD, AND DO AS YOU PLEASE."

THE LAST WEEK

Today is the day that we call Good Friday. What happened on this day that makes it good? Someone once asked me why they call it Good Friday? What is good about it?

Good Friday is a holy day celebrated by Christians on the Friday before Easter or Pascua

It commemorates the crucifixion of Jesus at Cavalry. Special prayer services are often held on this day with readings from the Gospels account of the events leading up to the crucifixion.

Easter always falls on Sunday between March 22 to April 25. **Easter** celebrates the Resurrection of Jesus Christ while **Lent** is a time of preparation for the Holy Week and holy days.

As we study the events leading up to the crucifixion we find that **Lent** begins with **Ash Wednesday.** There are 40 days between the beginning of Lent and Easter, not counting Sundays. Traditionally, during this time Christians observe the period marked by fasting, both from foods and festivities and perform other acts of penance. Fasting in the old times was more severe than it is today. Meat, fish, eggs and mil products were strictly forbidden and only one meal was eaten per day. Lent may have originated for practical reasons. In those days food stored in the previous autumn was running out or had to be rationed. Some foods needed to be used before it spoiled. Little or no new food crops were expected. In order to use up the food the people went on reduced rations. The British gardeners call it the "hungry gap."

In the Christian calendar we find a day called Shrove Tuesday. That is the day before Ash Wednesday. It is also known as Pancake Day. The word shrove comes from the English verb to schrive—which means to absolve the people from their sins. It is another way of using up the milk, eggs and flour prior to Lent.

The fourth Sunday of Lent was called **Laetare Sunday.** It marks the half way point between Ash Wednesday and Easter.

The Sunday before **Easter** is the beginning of **Holy Week** and we know it as the day that Jesus made his triumphal entry into Jerusalem through the Golden Gate. It also is known as Palm Sunday. As prophesied, he entered the city riding on a young colt and the people greeted him with palm branches. They expected the messiah to become the new King and free them from Roman bondage. In that last week Jesus cursed the fig tree, and cleansed the temple.

He was anointed and recognizes the sinister plots that developed that would send him to the cross. Acts of betrayal, cruelty, deceit, physical abuse and finally crucifixion lay ahead.

On Thursday of that week Jesus met with his disciples in the Upper Room and together they celebrated the Pass-Over Feast. At that time Jesus established the Lord's Supper. (see Matthew 26:17-29) This Thursday was known as **Maundy Thursday.**

Good Friday is a holy day celebrated by Christians which preserves the memory of the pain and suffering and the crucifixion of Jesus. He was treated like a criminal. He was purged beaten, mocked and scorned. He was rejected by the people he loved and served. He hung on the cross and died for our sins. What can we say was good about Good Friday? Simply that it is the day Jesus Christ gave his life for remission of our sins and that gives us the promise of eternal life.

"Whoever believes and is baptized will be saved, but whoever does not believe will be condemned." Mark 16:16.

Easter is the day that we celebrate the resurrection. As prophesied, Jesus arouse from the grave and proved that he is the Son of God. He defeated death that we might have hope in life.

MEMORIAL DAY CELEBRATION

Memorial Day was originally called **Decoration Day**. It is a day of remembrance for those who have died in our nation's service. There are many stories as to its actual beginnings, with over two dozen towns and cities claiming to be the birth place of **Memorial Day.**

There is evidence that there was an organized group of women from the South that were decorating graves before the end of the Civil War. A hymn written in **1867** entitled *"Kneel Where Our Loves are Sleeping"* by Nella L. Sweet, credits the ladies of the South for decorating the graves of the Confederate dead.

Memorial Day was officially proclaimed on May 5, 1868 by General John Logan, National Commander of the Grand Army of the Republic. General Logan's *General Order No. 11* was first observed on May 30, 1868 by placing flowers on the graves of both Union and Confederate soldiers at Arlington National Cemetery.

The first **State** to officially recognize the holiday was New York, in 1873. By 1890 it was recognized by all of the Northern states. The South states refused to acknowledge the day and honored their dead on separate days until after World War I (when the holiday changed from honoring those who died fighting in the Civil War to honoring all **Americans** who died fighting in any war).

Memorial Day is now celebrated by almost every State on the last Monday in May. A bill was enacted by Congress in 1971 that made it a three day weekend and a Federal Holiday.

In 1915, inspired by a poem, *"In Flanders Fields"*, by **John McCrae, Moina Michael,** wrote this verse:

**"We cherish too. The Poppy red.
That grows on fields where valor led,
It seems to signal to the skies
That blood of heroes never dies".**

Molina Michael conceived an idea to wear red poppies on **Memorial Day,** in honor of those who died serving the nation during war. She was the first to wear one and sold poppies to her friends and co-workers with the money going to benefit servicemen and their families who were in need,

Madam Guerin from France visiting the United States learned of this new custom and when she returned to France she began making artificial red poppies to raise money for war orphans and widows. The tradition spread to other countries in 1921.

Madam Guerin approached the VFW and they became the first veterans organization to sell poppies nationally.

Traditional observance of **Memorial Day** has diminished over the years. Many Americans have forgotten the meaning and traditions of Memorial Day. At many cemeteries the graves of the fallen are increasingly ignored and neglected. Most people no longer remember the proper flag etiquette for the day. Many people look to Memorial Day as a three day weekend holiday. There are still towns and cities that continue to hold Memorial Day parades and ceremonies. Our own Rhode Island Veterans Cemetery has a spectacular display of flags on Memorial Day. We should be proud.of our heritage and keep it alive.

In 1951 the **Boy Scouts of America** began placing flags on the grave sites of the servicemen and women in our national cemeteries.

What we need to do is to return the **solemn and sacred spirit** back to **Memorial Day** and make it our traditional day of observance. The day that we honor our fallen heroes.

In keeping with our **Memorial Day** discussion I would like to share with you these thoughts:

So that others may have life and dwell in peace, happiness and freedom.

In Flanders Fields

In Flanders Fields the poppies blow
Between the crosses, row on row,
That mark our place; and in the sky
The larks, still bravely singing fly,
Scarce heard amid the guns below.

We are the Dead, short days ago,
We lived, fell down, saw sunset glow,
Loved and were loved, and now we lie,
In Flanders Fields.

Take up our quarrel with the foe,
To you from failing hands we throw,
The torch; be yours to hold on high.
If ye break faith with us who die,
We shall not sleep, though poppies grow
In Flanders Fields.
John McCrae

Scripture: *"May the Lord direct your hearts into God's love and Christ's perseverance." 2 Thessalonians 3:5*

God Bless America—On This 4th Of July

Since our nation's founding, 230 years ago in 1776, in Philadelphia, Pennsylvania, Americans have turned to prayer for inspiration, strength and guidance. In times of trial, we ask God for wisdom, courage, direction and comfort. We offer thanks for the countless blessings God has provided. And, we thank God for sanctifying every human life by creating each of us in His image. As we observe this National Holiday this year we call upon the Almighty to continue to bless America and her people.

The **Declaration of Independence,** unanimously declared by the thirteen original colonies of the United States of America, was adopted by the Continental Congress on **July 4, 1776.** The task of getting the document signed began on August 2, 1776. Congress made sure that all of the states would have access to an authenticated copy of the declaration by ordering a special printing of multiple copies on January 18, 1777.

Since that time Americans have celebrated their independence on the 4th of July.

> The *Daily Alta California* wrote this about the 4th of July in **1855:**
> **"Hallowed be the day, forever bright its memory,**
> **In the heart of the Nation.**
> **Sing to it, poets,**
> **Shout to it, freemen,**
> **Celebrate it with bonfires, parades and triumphant assemblies."**

And we do. We gather together to watch and enjoy the firework displays. We have local parades and picnics. We often come together to listen to patriotic speakers and give thanks for our freedoms.

"Almighty God . . . . We make our earnest prayer that Thou wilt keep the United States in Thy holy protection, and that Thou wilt incline the hearts of the citizens to cultivate a spirit of subordination and obedience to government, and entertain a brotherly affection and love for one another and for their fellow citizens of the United States at large.

And finally, that thou wilt most graciously be pleased to dispose us all to do justice, to love mercy and to demean ourselves with that charity, humility and pacific temper of mind which were the characteristics of the Divine Author of our blessed religion, and without a humble imitation of whose example in these things we can never hope to be a happy nation.

Grant our supplication, we beseech Thee, through Jesus Christ our Lord Amen."—**George Washington**

The secret to a good sermon is to have a good beginning, and a good ending and have the two as close together as possible.—**George Burns**

> *"If my people who are called by my name, will humble themselves,*
> *And pray, and seek my face, and turn from their wicked ways,*
> *Then will I forgive their sins, and will heal their land."*
> 2 Chronicles 7:14

Closing Prayer

OUR VIEWS ON AGING

The book of Proverbs was written to give prudence to the simple, knowledge and direction to the young. Solomon is thought to be the author of Proverbs, but as we read further into the book we learn that Solomon wasn't the only author, there were probably a number of "wise men" who made contributions to the works. Most of Proverbs stems from the tenth century B.C. during the time of Israel's United Kingdom.

Proverbs is said to be a practical book dealing with the art of living, and it bases **WISDOM** solidly on the fear of the Lord. Proverbs is not only for the young but for all who seek a righteous life, serving God. We all would like to have **WISDOM.** Here is what the scripture have to say about that:

> *Blessed is the man who finds wisdom, the man who gains understanding,*
> *For she, wisdom, is more profitable than silver and yields better returns than gold.*
> *She is more precious than rubies; nothing you desire can compare with her.*
> *Long life is in her right hand; in her left hand are riches and honor*
> *Her ways are pleasant ways, and all her paths are peaceful.*
> *She is a tree of life to those who embrace her; those who lay hold of her will be blessed.*
> *Proverbs 3:12-18*

When I chose the title of this devotional **Our Views of Aging,** I asked myself what views do I have about the aging process. I asked my wife how old she was, and her reply was, "**I don't know, all I can remember is that I have had 73 birthdays.**" Aging is not a chronological matter, it is an attitude or mental state.

Bob Hope once said "I don't feel old. I don't feel anything until about noon, and then it is time for my nap."

Phyllis Diller said, "Maybe it's true that life begins at Fifty . . . . but everything else starts to wear out, fall apart or spread out."

Always remember: **"LIFE IS NOT MEASURED BY THE NUMBER OF BREATHS WE TAKE . . . . BUT BY THE MOMENTS THAT TAKE OUR BREATH AWAY."**

A Good Example Is Often The Best Sermon

George Burns, Comedian-Actor, Once Said, "**The Secret To A Good sermon is to have a good beginning and a good ending, and to have the two as close together as possible.**"

But, another example of a good sermon is one that teaches by example. We are more likely to identify and relate to the morale of the story if we can understand the principles involved.

> *"A gentle answer turns away wrath,*
> *But a harsh word stirs up anger."*
> Proverbs 15:1

Two friends were walking through the desert one day. At one point in the journey, they had a wicked argument and one friend slapped the other one in the face.

The one who got slapped was hurt, but without saying anything he wrote in the sand:

"Today my best friend slapped me in the face."

They kept on walking until they came to an oasis. The water was clear and inviting so they decided to take a bath and cool off. They took off their clothes and dove into the blue water.

As they splashed and bathed the one who had been slapped in the face got entangled in some weeds became mired down and started drowning. But, his friend saved him.

After he recovered from the near drowning he wrote on a stone:

"Today my best friend saved my life."

The man who had slapped and saved his best friend asked him, "After I hurt you, you wrote in the sand, and now you write on stone. Why?"

His friend replied, "**When someone hurts us we should write it down in the sand where the winds of forgiveness can blow it away.**

But when someone does something good for us we must engrave it in stone where no wind can ever erase it."

> Message: "Learn to write your hurts in the sand and to carve your benefits in stone."

They say that it takes a minute to find a special person; an hour to appreciate them; a day to love them; but an entire life to forget them.

A young minister noticed that Charlie had been absent from church for several Sundays so he decided to make a call on him at his home.

Charlie looked out the window and saw the Pastor coming up the walk and wondered how he was going to explain why he had not been in church. He could tell him that he has been sick. that his wife had passed away, the weather was just too darn cold to venture out. Or, the car wouldn't start. Whatever.

When the door bell rang, Charlie went to let the Pastor in. They exchanged greetings and Charlie invited the minister to come and sit by the big fire he had blazing in the open hearth. They each pulled a comfortable chair up to the fireplace, sat down and watched the fire burn. Not a word was spoken.

After a while the minister took some irons and reached into the fire and pulled a burning coal to one side. They both quietly watched the ember burn out. Then the minister pickup the coal and put it back into the main fire. It quickly blazed up and began to burn brightly.

The minister got up and without saying a word started toward the door. Charlie humbly said, "Thank you for that wonderful sermon. I will see you in church next Sunday."

> Message: "Sometimes that which is unsaid is more meaningful than the spoken word,"
> **"When words are many, sin is not absent, but he who holds his tongue is wise."**
> Proverbs 10:19

My wife had a very dear friend, a Christian Minister, teacher and pastor by the name of Murray Hunt. While Murray was going to school he was invited to take over a pulpit for a preacher who was going on a sabbatical one summer. Murray accepted the call and went to the church all enthused and excited about his witness.

It didn't take long for him to find out that the church was full of problems. He said that he tailored his sermons and Sunday messages to attempt to convey to the congregation their unrighteousness but it didn't work. He used very method that he knew.

Finally, the last Sunday came. This was to be his final sermon. Murray led the congregation through its worship hour and when time came for him to deliver the Sunday message, Murray in total frustration, stepped up to the pulpit, opened his bible and said, **"LOVE GOD, AND DO AS YOU PLEASE." Amen.** He closed his Bible and walked to the back of the church.

> Message: If you truly love God you will do His will and not
> your own.
> **"The path of life leads upward for the wise."**
> Proverbs 15:24

> **Thoughts To Ponder!**

> Thoughts to ponder:
> Think of three things . . . .
> Whence you came,
> Where you are going
> And to whom you must account.

> There is so much bad
> In the best of us.
> And so much good
> In the worst of us,
> That is doesn't behoove
> Any of us,
> To talk about the rest of us.

Closing prayer.

ROSH HASHANAH
THE FEAST OF THE TRUMPETS

Today is the 22nd of September If you are Jewish you know the meaning of this very important day. **Rosh Hashanah.** It is a day which occurs on the first and second day of Tishri. In the book of Leviticus we read: ***"In the seventh month, on the first of the month, there shall be a Sabbath for you, a remembrance with Shofar blasts, a holy convocation."*** Leviticus **23: 22-23** This special day is also known as the Feast of the Trumpets. The rams horn or the **Shofar** was blown from morning until night.

Rosh Hashanah literally means, "head of the year" or "first of the year." It is known as the Jewish New Year. The name is somewhat deceptive, because there is little similarity between **Rosh Hashanah,** one of the holiest days of the year for the Jews, and our **New Year,** which sometimes consists of midnight drinking bashes and TV football games.

There is, however, one important similarity between the Jewish New Year and the American one: Many Americans use the New Year as a time to plan a better life, making resolutions, etc. But, the Jewish New Year is a time to begin introspection, looking back at the mistakes of the past year and planning the changes to make in the year ahead.

No work is permitted on **Rosh Hashanah.** Much of the day is spent in the synagogue where regular daily liturgy is somewhat expanded. There is a special prayer book called the **Machzor.** The day is filled with prayer and reading from the holy book.

Another popular observance during this holiday is eating apples dipped in honey, symbolizing a wish for a sweet new year. Still another popular practice of the holiday is **Tashlikh** ("casting off"). The men walk to a flowing water, such as a creek or river on the afternoon of the first day and empty their pockets into the river, symbolically casting off their sins. We used to say,

"They are shaking the lint out of their pockets."

The religious services for the holiday focus on the concept of God's sovereignty.

Judaism has several different "new years" a concept which may seem strange at first, but think of it this way: American "new year" starts in January, but the new school starts in September, and many businesses have "fiscal years that start at various times.

In Judaism, **Nisan 1** is the new year for the purpose of counting the reign of Kings and months on the calendar. **Elul 1** (in August) is the new year for the tithing of animals, and

Shevat 15 (in February) is the new year for trees (determining when the first fruits can be eaten.) **Tishri 1** (**Rosh Hashanah**) is the new year for Sabbatical and Jubilee years.

After the exile the day was observed by the public reading of the Law and by general rejoicing.

Christians we are taught, and we realize, that we need to change and grow spiritually.

We don't have to wait until a special holiday is declared, but then sometimes that helps.

Christmas and Easter are special holidays that help us focus on our relationship with God and with each other. But as Paul writes to the Romans . . .

> "*. . . . we rejoice in the hope of the glory of God. Not only so, but we also rejoice in our sufferings, because we know that suffering produces perseverance; perseverance, character; and character, hope.*" Romans 5: 2-4

Paul suggests some basic things that we could do that would help to build our hopes is:

1. We need to remember that our troubles did not take God by surprise. HE is still in control.
2. Believe that God has a solution, a provision, or a gift of wisdom to match our problem.
3. Pray, affirming our faith in God and expressing our confidence is HIS loving purpose for us.
4. Wait with expectancy and availability, trusting God to work out HIS perfect will.
5. Praise HIM—even before HE acts.

One evening and old Cherokee Indian told his grandson about a battle that goes on inside of people . . . .

> He said, "My son, the battle is between two "**wolves**" inside each of us. One wolf is **Evil**, He is angry. He is envious, He is jealous, He is sorrowful,He is regretful, He is greedy, He is arrogant, He is full of resentment, He tellsLies, He is full of false pride. He is ego driven. **He is bad.**
>
> The other wolf is **Good**. He is joyful, He is at peace, He loves others, He has hope, He has serenity, He is humble, He is empathic, He is generous, He is truthful, and He is full of faith. **He is good.**
>
> The grandson thought for a moment and asked, **"Which wolf wins?"**
>
> The old Cherokee simply replied . . . ."**The one that you feed.**"

A TIME TO GIVE THANKS

In the book of Ecclesiastes, found in the Old Testament, we find some very important advice given to us by the writer who scholars think was Solomon. The writer outlines a formula for a **balanced life**, or perhaps he tells us **"What life is, not what it should be"**.

In Chapter 3, verse 1, he begins by saying, **"There is a time for everything, and a season for every activity under heaven."** He continues and reminds us that there is a time for everything that we experience, from birth until death, from laughter to tears. He also reminds us that,

"God has made everything beautiful in its time. He has also set eternity in the hearts of men; yet they cannot fathom what God has done from beginning to end. I know that there is nothing better for men than to be happy and do good while they live. That everyone may eat and drink, and find satisfaction in all of his toil — this is the gift of God" Eccl. 3 : 11-14

We are fortunate to have a time established by our government to nationally thank the Lord for that which we have through His bounty. We call that the time of **Thanksgiving. or Thanksgiving Day.**

In 1621, after a hard and devastating first year in the New World, the Pilgrim's fall harvest was very successful and plentiful. There was corn, fruits, vegetables, along with fish, which were packed in salt, and meat that was smoke cured over fires. They found enough food to put away enough for the next winter.

The Pilgrims had beaten the odds. They built homes in the wilderness, they raised enough crops to keep them alive during the coming winter, and they were at peace with their Indian neighbors.

Their **Governor, William Bradford,** proclaimed a day of thanksgiving that was to be shared by all of the colonist and the neighboring native American Indians.

The custom of an annually celebrated thanksgiving held after the harvest continued through the years. During the American Revolution (late

1770's) a day of national thanksgiving was suggested by the Continental Congress.

In 1817, New York State adopted **Thanksgiving Day** as an annual custom. By the middle of the 19 century many other states also celebrated a Thanksgiving Day. **In 1863**, President Abraham Lincoln proclaimed a national day of thanksgiving. Since that time each president has issued a Thanksgiving Day proclamation, usually designating the fourth Thursday of November as this special holiday This now is a time for giving thanks.

But how do we give thanks? The psalmist gives us some help, suggesting that we should:

> **"Shout for joy to the Lord, all the earth.**
> **Worship the Lord with gladness; come before Him with joyful songs.**
> **Know that the Lord is God. It is he who made us, and we are his.**
> **We are his people, the sheep of his pasture.**
> **Enter his gates with thanksgiving and his courts with praise.**
> **Give thanks to him and praise his name.**
> **For the Lord is good and his love endures forever;**
> **His faithfulness continues through all generations." Ps. 100**

God likes to hear from us. We can talk with him at any time at any place and for as long as we want. We call it **prayer.** But some people say, **I don't know how to pray . . . how do I do it?** Let me share with you a little crutch that you can use to help you pray.

The Five Finger Prayer.

1. Your thumb is nearest you. So begin your prayer with it. **Pray for those closest to you. They are the easiest to remember.**
2. The next finger is the pointing finger. **Pray for those who teach, instruct, heal. And advise, including teachers, doctors and ministers. They need help pointing others in the right direction.**

3. The next finger is the tallest finger. It reminds us of our leaders. **Pray for the President, the leaders of our country and the leaders of business and industry**

4. The fourth finger is the ring finger. Surprisingly this is the weakest finger . . . . ask any piano teacher. It reminds us to **Pray for those who are weak, in trouble and in pain.**

5. And last . . . . comes our little finger, our pinky. The smallest finger reminds us where to place ourselves in relation to God and others. The **Bible** says: **"The least shall be the greatest among you."** Our little finger should remind us to pray for ourselves.

By the time we have prayed for the other four groups our own needs will be put in proper perspective and we will be able to pray for ourselves more effectively.

Pray a prayer using the five finger crutch.

THE TRUE MEANING OF CHRISTMAS

What is the true meaning of Christmas? As we approach another Christmas Season we look around, wonder and question the way people prepare to celebrate the birth of our Savior, Jesus Christ, and how they inter—act with one another.

Recently I read an article in the local paper about how stores are trying **anger management** to deal with stressed shoppers. "**Tis the season to be angry.**" The countdown to Christmas has dwindled to a few days and the mall crowds have gotten stressed trying to buy the right gift. They are taking it out on the clerks and the sales people as well as their fellow shoppers. There are reports of people fighting over merchandise, wresting each other is the aisles and even shooting each other. They start out with the best intentions of celebrating the holiday, buying gifts for their family and friends and then they get caught up in the frenzy and things get out of control. This can't be something that God has intended.

Then we have the folks who declare that this Christmas is going to be different. No Christmas cards to write, no long list of presents to buy, no over spending and runaway credit card debt, that will take until August to pay off. Just bake a few cookies, decorate the tree and turn on the candles in the window. Maybe even have a couple of relatives in for dinner Christmas Day. **This is Christmas!** Sound familiar?

Oh, but don't try to put a nativity scene on the Town Hall lawn, or to even greet each other with a **Merry Christmas,** and to sing a jolly Christmas Carole, don't do it, it might offend our non-Christian neighbors who will want to take you to court,.

So, what is the true meaning of Christmas and how do we go about celebrating this wonderful gift from God?

The answer is **LOVE**—that is the true meaning of Christmas.

John 3:16-17 says,
"For God so loved the world, that he gave His only begotten Son,
That whosoever believes in Him should not perish, but have
everlasting life
For God sent not his Son into the world to condemn the world,
but that
The world through Him might be saved."

The true meaning of Christmas is **Love.** God loved us so much that He wanted to provide a way for us to spend eternity with Him. He gave His only Son to take the punishment for our sins. He paid the price in full. We are free from condemnation when we accept that free gift of **LOVE.**

Why did God do such a thing? Because He loves us! Why was Christmas necessary? Because we needed a Savior. Why does God love us so much? **Because He is Love!**

1 John 4:8 says,
"Whoever does not love does not know God, because God is LOVE."

Someone once said, "If God had a refrigerator he would have our picture on it."

"And He would certainly have our photo in His wallet."

Why do we celebrate Christmas every year? Out of gratitude for what God did for us, We remember Jesus' birth by giving each other gifts, worshipping Him, and being especially conscious of the poor and less fortunate.

Certainly there are many ways that we can celebrate Christmas. I proclaim that we should include Jesus, and the Love that God has for us, as basic and essential in all that we do. Let us be aware of the less fortunate and the poor to share God's love.

God's Christmas Present

Let me tell you the story of the sweet Jesus Christ,
Who brought heaven to earth one cold winter night?

As planned by His father, a long time ago.
      In the form of a babe, he came down below.

His divine mission unknown at the time,
Was later revealed, when God felt inclined.

The day the sweet Lord was nailed to the cross,
Was the day that God showed mankind was not lost

By the Son's grief and pain, man could be forgiven.
And God gave to us a vision of heaven.

But thick in his thinking, and blind in his heart,
Man missed the Lord's meaning, and remained in the dark.

Thus, each year at Christmas, the tale is retold.
And man is reminded of Jesus Christ's role.

Access to heaven, God's gift to man,
God's Christmas present, the start of His plan

      Sent by the Father from Heaven above,
      Truly a message of God's everlasting Love.

WHAT IS THE PRICE?

How often do we learn of a story that clearly and succinctly tells us what we need to know?

Maybe not often enough. This story provides a very clear lesson. This is one of those stories.

Once there was a man named George Thomas, a pastor, in a small New England town. One Sunday morning he came to church carrying a rusty. bent, old bird cage and sat it on the pulpit. The members of the congregation wondered what he was going to say.

Eyebrows were raised, and as if in response, the Pastor Thomas began to speak . . . He said. "I was walking through town yesterday when I saw a young boy coming towards me swinging this bird cage. On the bottom of the cage were three little wild birds, shivering with cold and frightened almost to death. I stopped the lad and asked, "What have you got in the cage son?" **"Just some old birds,"** came the reply.

"What are you going to do with them?" asked the pastor. "Take 'em home and have fun with 'em," the boy answered. "I'm gonna **tease 'em** and **pull out their feathers,** and make 'em fight. I'm gonna have a real good time." "But you'll get tired of those birds sooner or later. Then what will you do?" asked the preacher.

Oh, I got some cats. said the boy. They like birds. I'll just give 'em to them.

The pastor was silent for a moment and then said, "How much do you want for those birds, son?

Huh! You don't want them birds, mister. They are just plain old field birds. They don't sing, they don't do anything, they ain't even pretty. The pastor asked again, "How much?" The boy sized up the pastor as if he were crazy, and said, "$10.00."

The pastor reached into his pocket and took out a ten dollar bill. He placed it in the boy's hand and in a flash the boy was gone.

The pastor gently carried the cage to the alley where there was a tree, put the cage down, opened the door and coaxed the little birds to come out. He placed them in the tree setting them free.

That explained the empty cage that was on the pulpit. But the pastor began to tell the rest of the story: He said:

"One day Satan and Jesus were having a conversation. Satan had just come from the Garden of Eden and he was gloating and boasting "Yes sir, I just caught me a world full of people down there. I set a trap, used bait they couldn't resist. I call it **SIN**. Got them all, every one of them."

"What are you going to do with them?" asked Jesus. "Oh, I'm gonna have fun with them," Satan replied. "I'm going to teach them to marry and divorce each other, how to hate and abuse each other, how to lie and cheat on each other, how to drink and smoke and curse. I'm gonna teach them how to invent **guns** and **bombs** and how to kill each other. I'm really gonna have fun."

"And what will you do when you get done with them?" Jesus asked. "Oh, I'll kill them and let them **burn in Hell**," Satan glared proudly.

"How much do you want for them?" Jesus asked.

"Oh, you don't want those people. They ain't no good. If you take them they will hate you. They will spit you, curse you and crucify you. You don't want those people."

How much? Jesus asked.

Satan looked at Jesus and sneered, **"All your blood, your tears and your life!"**

Jesus smiled and said, "DONE." And he paid the price.

The pastor picked up the cage, opened the door and walked out of the church.

Prayer

NEW YEAR'S RESOLUTIONS

The third Monday in January reported to be the **"Bluest Day of the Year"**. A psychologist from Cambridge University in England declared that the third Monday in January is the worst time for depression and he called it the **"Bluest Day of the Year." Depression** is defined "As the time when people do without the things their parents never had."

The third Monday in January was chosen because:
1. The Christmas holiday and New Year's partying is over.
2. The weather is probably at its worst, cold, snowing and nasty.
3. The bills that we charged on our credit cards have arrived, and need to be paid. We have very likely broken all of our New Year's resolutions. So be it.

As a culture, we do not celebrate January 1st out of some Judean-Christian obligation.

Instead, we wave off the pagan cloud that hangs over many New Year rituals and we pause to thank God for another year of life and another year of sacred promises.

The practice of making New Year's Resolutions goes back over 3000 years to the ancient

Babylonians. There is something about the start of the New Year that gives us the feeling of a fresh start and a new beginning. In reality, there is nothing sacred about December 31st ^{a}nd January 1. Nothing mystical occurs at midnight New Year's Eve. And, what is wrong with making a New Year's Resolution on January 26? If a Christian decides to make a

New Year's Resolution then we should go ahead and do it. The question is how should it be done?

Common New Year's Resolutions are: **to quit smoking, quit drinking, manage money better, and spend more time with the family.** Most common resolutions include, **losing weight, exercising more and eating healthier.** These are all good goals to set. However,

1 Timothy 4:8 instructs us to keep exercise in perspective: "**Bodily exercise is all right, but spiritual exercise is far more important and is a tonic for all that you do**".

> The Jewish prophet Micah rallies us in the direction of renewed character. Micah asks.
>
> **"What does the Lord require of you? To act justly, to love mercy and to walk humbly with God."**

According to a CNN survey of 12,000 Americans taken in 2005, 70% of us break our resolutions by February 1. That means we have only a few more days to go. You may not have made a single resolution this year. On the other hand, you may have intended to make a resolution but didn't. Or, you may have made several resolutions and have been faithful in keeping them all.

Philippians 4:13 tells us, **"I can do everything through Him who gives me strength."**

The practice of making New Year's Resolutions goes back over 3000 years to the ancien Babylonians. There is something about the start of the New Year that gives us the feeling of a fresh start and a new beginning. In reality, there is nothing sacred about December 31st ªnd January 1. Nothing mystical occurs at midnight on New Year's Eve. And, what is wrong with making a New Year's Resolution on January 26? If a Christian decides to make a New Year's Resolution then we should go ahead and do it. The question is how should it be done?

The Jewish prophet Micah rallies us in the direction of renewed character. Micah asks.

"What does the Lord require of you? To act justly, to love mercy and to walk humbly with God."

The following words are chiseled in the gateway at the United States Naval Academy at Annapolis: **"The measure of a man is the depth of his convictions, the breadth of his interests and the height of his ideals."** The same goes for any person, family, or nation.

Philippians 4:13 tells us, **"I can do everything through Him who gives me strength."**

John 15:5 declares, **"I am the vine, you are the branches. If a man remains in me and I in him, he will bear much fruit."** If God is the center of your resolution it has a good chance for success, depending on your commitment to it. If it is God's will for something to be fulfilled, He will enable you to fulfill it. If the resolution is not God honoring or is not in agreement with God's Word, we will not received God's help.

If we are going to **"look up"** in the coming year we need to focus on our walk with God, not on keeping up with the Joneses.

If we going to **"look down"** in this year let us not see our cup as half empty, but consider the people of the world who live on less that $2 per day and have much less than we have.

If we are going to **"look out"** during the year we need to remember the words of Mother Teresa, who said, "We cannot do great things . . . . only small thing with great love."

So, what sort of resolution should a Christian make and how should we do it?

(1) Pray to the Lord for wisdom in regards to what you should resolve.

(2) Pray for wisdom as to how to fulfill the goals that God gives you.

(3) Rely on God's strength to help you.

(4) Find an accountability partner who will help you and encourage you.

(5) Don't be proud or vain, give God the glory.

"Commit your way to the LORD, trust also in Him, and He shall bring it to pass."
Psalms 37: 5

Prayer

HAPPY MOTHER'S DAY

Mother's Day is a holiday honoring mothers. It is not a religious holiday, per se, but it is celebrated in many places around the world. It is a day on which we honor our mothers.

William M. Thackery said, "**Mother**, is the name for God in the lips and hearts of little children."

Mother's Day is celebrated on the 2nd Sunday in May in the United States and Canada.

Mothers often receive gifts on this day. According to the National Restaurant Association, Mother's Day is now the most popular day of the year to dine out at a restaurant.

I can remember my mother saying to my father and my sister and brother, **"Tomorrow the kitchen will be closed . . . . we will be eating out . . . it is Mother's Day."** That was our clue to knowing about Mother's Day. And so it was.

Different countries celebrate Mother's Day on various days of the year because the holiday has a number of different origins. One thought is Mother's Days emerged from a custom of mother worship in ancient Greece. The Greeks kept a festival to **Cybele**, a great mother of gods, and mythology. She was the wife of **Coronus,** and the festival was held around the Vernal Equinox. In Rome the festival was held from the **Ides of March** (March 15 to March 18). The Romans also had another holiday, **Matronalia,** which was dedicated to Juno, and mothers were usually given gifts on this day.

The United States copies Mother's Day from England, and it was introduced after the American Civil War by Julia Ward Howe who was a social activist. Her mission was uniting women against war. She is famous for having written the Mother's Day Proclamation. If she were alive today she would be considered a liberal anti war monger.

In 1858 a young woman from Appalachia, by the name of Ann Jarvis, organized women to work for improved sanitation, she called her efforts Mother's Work Days. Her mission was fruitful and in her memory, in parts of the United States, it is customary to plant tomatoes outdoors after mother's day (but not before).

When Ann Jarvis died her daughter Anna Jarvis started a crusade to found a memorial day for women. The first such Mother's Day was celebrated in Grafton, West Virginia on May 20, 1908, and the custom caught on. Each of the 50 states and Canada observe the second Sunday in May as *Mother's Day.*

The Bible says, *"Train up a child in the way he should go and when he is old, he will not depart from it."* Proverbs 22:6

A story: A mother was worried about her kindergarten son walking to school.

He didn't want his mother to walk with him. She wanted to give him some feeling of independence, but she needed to know that he was safe.

She had an idea. She would ask her neighbor to follow him but to stay at a distance so she wouldn't be noticed. The neighbor agreed because she liked to get up early and exercise by walking. The next day the neighbor and her toddler daughter, followed behind Johnny and his friend as they walked to school. She did this for a whole week.

As the boys walked and chatted, kicking stones and twigs, Johnny's friend noticed the lady and little girl following them and finally said, "Have you. seen that lady following us to school all week? Do you know her?"

Johnny nonchalantly replied, "Yeah, I know her."

"Well, who is she?" his friend asked.

"That is **Shirley Goodnest**," Johnny replied, "And her daughter **Marcy.**"

"Shirley Goodnest? Who the heck is she and why is she following us?"

Well, Johnny explained, "Every night my Mom and I say the 23rd Psalm with my prayers, cuz she worries about me so much. And in the 23rd Psalm, it says,

'**Shirley Goodnest and Marcy shall follow me all of the days of my life**'
So I guess I'll just have to get used to it."

In Proverbs 31:28 we read, *"Her children arise and call her blessed; her husband also, and he praises her."*

> *"The Lord bless you and keep you;*
> *The Lord make his face to shine upon you,*
> *And be gracious unto you:*
> *The Lord lift His countenance upon you*
> *And give you peace."*
> Numbers 6:24-26

And **may Shirley Goodnest and Marcy be with you today and always.**

HAVE A HAPPY AND BLESSED MOTHER'S DAY!

What Is Ash Wednesday?

Ash Wednesday is the day that **Lent** begins. **Ash Wednesday** is not a *holy day of obligation* but many people would not think of letting Ash Wednesday go by without a trip to church to be marked with an ashen cross on their foreheads. Even people who seldom go to Church for the rest of the year may make a concerted effort to come for ashes.

The official name of Ash Wednesday is the **"The Day of Ashes"**. The reason the day became known as Ash Wednesday is that it is forty days before **Good Friday,** and will always be on a Wednesday. The Bible does not mention either Lent or Ash Wednesday, but. the Bible does tell of the acts of repentance and supplication that were made by God fearing people.

The period of Lent is intended to be a time when sinful activities and habits are forsaken. **Ash Wednesday** is the "commencement" of this period of repentance. Perhaps you can remember some acts of repentance that you did. You may have given up eating ice cream or having a smoke, or drinking a beer, giving up going to the popular Friday Night movie, or eating that favorite dessert. And you were very compliant. Forty days is a long time.

The Bible contains numerous accounts of people using "dust and ashes" as a symbol of repentance and/or mourning. One example is Daniel, God's prophet who said:

> *"Then I turned to the Lord God and prayed and asked Him for help. I did not eat any food. To show my sadness I put on rough cloth and sat in ashes. I prayed to the Lord my God and told him about all of my sins." Daniel 9:3*

At the beginning of the 11th century it became a custom for all of the faithful to take part in a ceremony on the Wednesday before Lent that included the imposition of ashes.

The tradition is that the sign of the cross is made in ashes on a person's forehead as a symbol of that person's identification with Jesus Christ. h Wednesday, along with Lent is observed by most Roman Catholics, most Orthodox denominations and a few Protestant denominations. Since the Bible does not command or condemn the procedure, a Christian is at liberty to prayerfully decide whether to observe **AsWednesday** or not. If you feel led to the Lord to observe Ash Wednesday and/or Lent the important thing is to have a Biblical perspective. It is good to repent of sinful activities.

It is good to clearly identify yourself as a Christian. But we should not believe that God will automatically bless us in response to the observing of a ritual.

God is interested in our hearts, not in our doing rituals.

Remember that God loves us because of **who God is**, not because of **anything we did or did not do.**

Three things in Life that, once they are gone never come back:
1. Time
2. Words
3. Opportunity.

Three things in life that are never certain are:
1. Fortune
2. Success
3. Dreams

Three things that make a person significant are:
1. Commitment
2. Sincerity
3. Hard work

Three things that are truly "Constant" are: *FATHER,—SON—HOLY SPIRIT.*

"I ask the Lord to bless you, as I prayed for you today,
To guide you and protect you, as you go along your way.
God's love is always with you, God's promises are true,
And when you give God all your cares,
You know that God will see you through."

Life is not about waiting for the storm to pass . . . It's about learning how to dance in the rain.

ST. VALENTINE'S DAY

When we think of Valentine's Day we are conditioned to think of **Cupid, Candy, Lacy Hearts and Bouquets of Flowers, Fancy Cards** and a **Holiday,** devoted to romantic love. Isn't it interesting that one of the best known Christian saints, on the secular calendar, was a martyr for the Christian faith? St. Valentine's Day is not *Eros, romantic or sexual love,* but rather *Agape, selfless love for others and for God.*

There were three different Saint Valentines, all of them martyrs, mentioned in the early martyrologies for the date February 14th. One was a priest in Rome, another a bishop (of modern Terni) and the third was a martyr in Africa. Little is known about these early Christian men, except that, "**Each died for the love of Christ.**

The Golden Legend, a medieval book of stories about saints tells of a priest, **Valentine,** who was imprisoned by the Emperor Claudius II for leading people to Christ. While

Valentine was being interrogated by a Roman officer, the priest preached **Christ** as the "One and Only Light". The officer who had a blind daughter, challenged Valentine to pray to Christ for his daughter's cure. The girl was cured, and the entire family was converted to Christianity. According to legend, while awaiting execution, Valentine wrote notes of instruction, affection and encouragement to the Christian community in Rome, and they were secretly delivered by a young boy who visited him in prison.

When we realize that the heart of Saint Valentine was, like other Christian martyrs, "pierced" by the love of Our Lord Jesus Christ, and that he shed his blood for this, it seems appropriate that the **red heart** is a symbol of this powerful love. We think about the power of the love of God—our love for Him—and His for us—and it inspires us to love one another. It is this kind of love that encourages the faithful Christian to accomplish deeds of extra-ordinary courage, even unto death, to bring the truth of faith to others.

On St. Valentine's Day, we Christians have an opportunity for some real **inculturation,** that is planting seeds of Christ's truth into the cultures in which we live.

The popular customs of St. Valentine's Day probably originated in medieval Europe. It was common belief in England and France that on February 14th, which is half way through the second month of the year, the birds began to pair. This fostered a belief that "love birds" represented the day dedicated to lovers, and provided the proper occasion for writing love letters and sending lover's tokens. There are many examples that can be used to illustrate Valentine's Day. But, never forget what the Bible says and the teachings of our Savior Jesus Christ.

There are many passages of the Bible that reflect God's love. One of the best known is **John 3:16:** *"For God so loved the world that he gave his only begotten Son, that whosoever believeth on Him should not perish, but have everlasting life."*

THE TELEPHONE RUNAROUND

Psalm 34:15-22

Everyone who owns a personal computer has, or will have, to call their carrier for help some day. Computers seem to get the "virus" more often than people and when the computer gets sick, it is serious. It was my turn last week when I discovered that I couldn't access the internet.

First came the task of finding the telephone number. Then the number was dialed followed by several busy signals. When the phone was finally answered, it was a computerized voice saying, "Press 1 for English, 2 for Spanish". I selected 1. Then it asked for my ten digit telephone number, which I punched in. Next, it asked if I wanted Sales, new programs or up grades, if so, press 1; if I needed Accounting I was instructed to press 2; and if I needed Technical Service press 3. I pressed 3, the phone rang once and the voice came on and started me back through the maize again, from the very beginning.

When I finally reached the Service Department, I was required to give them my Mother's Maiden name, the last four digits of my social security number and the account number for my service, I was connected to the same sweet computer voice that lead me through the initial maize and it asked me about the trouble I was having. Twenty minutes later, after I had shut down the computer, disconnected the modem, and unplugged the unit I was told to re-boot the system. I did, and the problem didn't go away. After another 30 minutes I finally was able to talk to a real live person who asked for all of my personal information again.

While I struggled through this exercise, I thought about the need to talk to the Lord. I knew I wouldn't get a busy signal. I knew I wouldn't be put on hold, and I knew I didn't have to remember my social security number. I knew that God was listening and He cared deeply for me.

We don't always get immediate answers to our prayers, but because of the wonderful prayer promises in the Bible we know that we are heard. In

Psalms 34. David reviewed his prayers and the Lord's answers. And then he said, *"The eyes of the Lord are on the righteous, and His ears are open to their cry." Psalm 34:15*

Thank God that there is no such thing as a prayer runaround. We have a direct line to God. All we have to do is learn to use it.

Amen

WHAT KIND OF MAN WOULD DO SUCH A THING?

At Walter Reed Medical Center in Washington, DC. recently the Sergeant Major of the Army, Jack Tilley, was with a group of people visiting the wounded soldiers.

He saw a Special Forces soldier who had lost his right hand and suffered severe wounds to his face and side of his body. The Sergeant Major wanted to honor him and show him respect without offending him. But what can you say or do in such a situation that will encourage and uplift? How do you shake the right hand of a soldier who has none?

There was a man in the group of visitors who had his wife with him, also visiting the soldiers. He seemed to know exactly what to do. The man reverently took the soldier's stump of a hand in both of his hands, knelt at the bedside and prayed for him. When he finished the prayer, he stood up, bent over the soldier and kissed him on the head, and told him that he loved him. A powerful expression of love and a Christ-like example for one of our wounded heroes.

What kind of man would do such a thing? The wounded man's Commander-in-Chief, George W. Bush, President of the United States of America.

God bless the President and everyone in the USA.

THE REFINER OF SILVER

Malachi 3:3 says: "He will sit as a refiner and purifier of silver."

This verse in Malachi puzzled some members of a Bible study and they wondered what this statement meant, about the character and nature of GOD.

One of the ladies in the group offered to find out the process of refining silver and she promised to get back to the group at their next meeting.

That week the woman made an appointment to watch a silversmith at work. She didn't mention anything about the reason for her interest. As she watched him she noticed that the craftsman held a piece of silver over the fire and let it heat up. He explained that in refining silver one needed to hold the silver in the middle of the fire where the flames were the hottest so as to burn away all of the impurities.

The woman thought about GOD holding us in such a hot spot, then she thought again about the verse that says: **"He sits as a refiner and purifier of silver."** She asked the silversmith if it was necessary that to sit there in front of the fire the whole time the silver was being refined?

The man answered **"Yes."** He not only had to sit there holding the silver, but he had to keep his eyes on the silver the entire time it was in the fire. If the silver was left in the flames a moment too long it would burn up and be destroyed.

The woman was silent for a moment. Then she asked the silversmith, "How do you know when the silver is fully refined?" He smiled at her and answered, "Oh that is easy—when I see my image in it."

If we are feeling the heat of the fire, remember that GOD has his eye on us and will keep watching us until He sees His image.

Like the silver, whatever we are going through, we will be better persons in the end.

Closing Prayer

WHO SEES OUR WORTH?

"Our hearts may condemn us." With those words, the Bible acknowledges that at times our heart may cause us to be overly critical of ourselves. Indeed, it may insist that we are unworthy of God's love and care. Yet, the Bible reassures us: **"God is greater than our hearts and knows all things." 1 John 3:19, 20.**

God knows us better than we know ourselves. He views us in a very different way, than the way we view ourselves. What then are we worth in the eyes of the one who really matters—Jehovah God?

The answer can be found in a touching illustration that Jesus used on two separate occasions.

Jesus said that, "Two sparrows sell for a coin of small value**." (Matthew 10:29, 31.)**

According to **Luke 12: 6,7,** Jesus also said: *"Five sparrows sell for two coins of small value,"* yet not one of them goes forgotten before God . . . . *"Have no fear, you are worth more than many sparrows"* This simple but powerful illustration teaches us how God views each of His worshippers.

In Biblical time sparrows were among the cheapest of all birds used for food. Jesus observed poor women, perhaps even his own mother, in the marketplace buying these tiny birds to feed to their families. The birds were so inexpensive that for two coins, **one coin was worth less than five cents in modern value,** a buyer could purchase two sparrows. For two coins the buyer received not four but five sparrows at no additional cost.

Jesus explained that not a single sparrow goes forgotten before God, or falls to the ground without the Father's knowledge. (Matthew 10:29) The seemingly insignificant birds that were not too little for Jehovah to create are not too little for Him to remember. In fact He values them, for they are, precious living things. And so it is with us.

As we look to our modern time there seems to be a paradox . . . that is:

As we spend more, we have less.
We buy more but don't have as much.
We have bigger houses and smaller families.
There are more conveniences but less time.
There are more medicines but less wellness.
We read too little, and watch TV too much.
And we pray too seldom.

We have multiplied our possessions, but reduced our values.
These seem be times of tall men with short characters.
There are steep profits, and shallow relationships.
These are days of two incomes, but more divorces.
Fancier houses but broken homes.
We have learned how to make a living, but not a life.
We've added years to life, but not life to years.
We've cleaned up the air, but polluted the soul.
We want to be independent without acknowledging that God
has made us and we are His children.

In light of Jesus' words, we need not feel that we are too unworthy to be noticed and cared for by the God who is **"greater than our hearts."** Isn't it comforting to know that our Creator may see **in us** what we may not be able to see in ourselves?

We need to know that we will not be remembered by our words, but by our kind deeds.

Life is not measured by the breathes we take but by the moments that take our breath.

Closing prayer

RICHARD K. STENMARK

1937-2007
Reflections and Memories

I was honored to meet and get to know Richard Stenmark here at the First Baptist Church of East Greenwich. The first Sunday that I saw him was when I gave the Children's story using the Learjet model. Richard was my best audience, he seemed fascinated with aviation and he never let me forget it.

One of the things that I will always remember are the visits we had at the hospitals and nursing homes. I was kidding him not long ago about how one needed to be a super sleuth in order to keep up with him as he moved from one place to the other.

Richard was very appreciative of the members of the church. Their cards and letters and many visits were rays of sunshine for him.

We talked about many things and we would often have Communion. He always asked if we could have a moment of prayer before we departed.

A visit with Richard seemed like he was calling on me, rather than me calling on him. Living a life that matters doesn't happen by accident. It's not a matter of circumstances but of choice.

Richard enjoyed the essence of life. It must have been frustrating and difficult for him to be confined to a bed after having been a person of mobility and energy for so many years.

I would like to think that since I saw him last he has continued his march to Zion.

"Nothing in all creation is hidden from God's sight. Everything is uncovered and laid bare before the eyes of Him to whom we give account" Hebrews 4:13

MEMORIES OF MEMORIAL DAY

When we look at pictures of Memorial Day we usually see cemeteries like Arlington National Cemetery with thousands of pristine markers in unbroken waves, or the cemetery at Normandy with its countless crosses and stars of David. And it is good.

One memory I have of Memorial Day is the beautiful cemetery in Springfield, Illinois, named Oak Ridge. Abraham Lincoln's tomb is the center piece of this memorial garden. My grand—father, my grandmother, aunt Esther, my uncle Ben, and my wife and infant son are resting there. And, as a young Boy Scout, I remember how our Scout Master, Ted Brown would have all of the members of our troop put American Flags on every veteran's grave.

In addition to being our Scout Master, Ted Brown was a member of the American Legion and he believed that we should honor our war veterans. Ted volunteered to do this every year.

At the end of the day we would scatter through the area, in the day's waning light, to collect the flags before sunset. We found flags at the feet of the most ornate marble angels or next to a simple granite stone. Some of the graves had pretty rose bushes around them, or fresh flowers in vases nearby. Others were neglected and overgrown, as though no one had visited in years.

Most of the flags were for people I'd never known, some of whom had died all too young. But like Ted Brown said, "They are veterans who sacrificed their lives for freedom and we need to honor them this way."

By sunset the flags were put away in boxes and bags and placed in the back of Ted's car ready for next Memorial Day. We would dash home tired but pleased with our efforts.

We all had learned that remembering the dead wasn't **passive.** It was something that Scout Master Brown did year after year and the lesson that was learned was that we owed thanks to generation after generation in graves, plain and fancy, known and unknown, for what they had done for us.

We need to keep **that solemn and sacred spirit of Memorial Day. We ne**ed to make it our traditional day of observance. The day that we honor our fallen heroes. The day that we praise God and thank Him for granting us our Freedom.

One traditional is the selling of poppy flowers by members of the Veterans of Foreign Wars.

Scripture:

> **I lift up my eyes to the hills—**
> **where does my help come from?**
> **My help comes from the Lord,**
> **the maker of heaven and earth.**
> **He will not let your foot slip—**
> **he who watches over you will not slumber; . . . .**
> **The Lord watches over you . . .**
> **the Lord is your shade at your right hand;**
> **The sun will not harm you by day,**
> **nor the moon by night.**
> **The Lord will keep you from all harm—**
> **he will watch over your life;**
> **The Lord will watch over your coming and going**
> **both now and forevermore.**
> **Psalm 121:1-3, 5-8**

Traditionally we need to acknowledge and praise God for having allowed us the freedom that we enjoy. Psalm 119:45-48 explains:

> **I will walk about in freedom for I have sought out your precepts.**

I will speak of your statutes before kings and not be put to shame, for I delight in your commands because I love them.

I lift up my hands to your commands, which I love, and I meditate on your decrees.

Closing prayer.

A Time To Sow And A Time To Reap

The Book of Ecclesiastes is found in the Old Testament. There doesn't seem to be a specific time period and the writer's name is not mentioned in the book. But several passages strongly suggest that **King Solomon** is the author and it was written near the end of his life.

In all of **King Solomon's** wisdom, he takes stock of the world as he has experienced it, between the *horizons of birth and death,*—the latter a horizon beyond which man cannot see. The world is full of enigmas, the greatest of which is man himself.

King Solomon looks at human enterprise, he sees man in mad pursuit of one thing and then another—laboring as if he could master the world, lay bare its secrets, change its fundamental structures, break through the bounds of human limitations and master his own destiny.

But *faith* teaches us that God has ordered all things according to his own purpose and that man's role is to accept these, including our own limitations, as God's appointments. Man therefore, should be patient and enjoy life as God gives it. We should be prudent in everything that we do, living carefully before God, fearing Him and keeping his commandments

Scripture: Eccl. 7:8 "The end of a matter is better than its beginning, And patience is better than pride."

Having said that, I am reminded of a story of a discussion that God was having with St. Francis.

GOD: "Frank, you know all about gardens and nature. What in the world is going on down there on planet Earth What has happened to the dandelions, the violets, the thistle and stuff that I starter eons ago? I had a perfect no-maintenance garden.

Those things would grow in any type of soil, with little water, and multiply with abandon.

Now all that I see are green rectangles."

St. Francis: It's man Lord. The Suburbanites. They started calling your flowers **"weeds"** and have gone to great lengths to kill them and replace them with grass."

God: "Grass." But it is so boring. It's not colorful. It doesn't attract butterflies, birds and bees; only grubs and worms. It's sensitive to temperatures. Do these Suburbanites really want all that grass growing there?"

St. Francis: Apparently so Lord. They go to great pains to grow it and keep it green.

They begin each spring by fertilizing grass and poisoning any other plants that crop up in the lawn.

God: "The spring rains and warm temperatures probably make grass grow quickly.

That must make the Suburbanites happy."

St. Francis: Apparently not Lord. As soon as it grows a little they cut it. Sometimes twice a week."

God: "They cut it? Do they bail it like hay?"

St. Francis: "Not exactly Lord, Most of them rake it up and put it in bags.

God: They bag it? Why? Is it a cash crop? Do they sell it?"

St. Francis: "No Sir, just the opposite. They pay to throw it away."

God: "Now let me get this straight. They fertilize the grass so it will grow, and when it does grow they cut it off and pay to throw it away . . . . They must be relieved in the summer when we cut back on the rain and turn up the heat. That surely slows the growth and saves them a lot of work."

St. Francis: "No, not really. When the grass stops growing so fast, they drag out hoses and pay more money to water it so they can continue to mow it and pay to get rid of it."

God: "What nonsense. At least they kept some of the trees. That was sheer stroke of genius, if I do say so myself. The trees grow leaves in the spring to provide beauty and shade in the summer. In the Autumn the leaves fall to the ground and form a natural blanket to keep the soil moist and protect the trees and bushes. It's a natural cycle of life."

St. Francis: "The Suburbanites have a new system. After the leaves fall, they rake them up into great piles and pay to have them hauled away. Then, in order to protect the shrubs and tree roots in the winter they go out and buy something the call **mulch.** They haul it home and spread it around in place of the leaves." "And they get the **mulch** from trees that they cut down and grind up."

God: "Enough . . . I don't want to think about it anymore".

We can all identify with the grass and leaves story. But isn't it an example of our wants to break through the bounds of our limitations and master our own destiny?

Finally, let's take a look on how to plant a garden. **First, you come to the valley alone, while the dew is still on the roses . . . .**

For a garden of daily living Plant three rows of Peas:

Peace of mind, peace of heart and peace of soul.

Plant four rows of squash:

Squash gossip, squash indifference, squash grumbling and squash selfishness.

Plant four rows of Lettuce:

Lettuce be faithful, lettuce be kind, lettuce be patient, lettuce really love one another.

No Garden is complete without Turnips:

Turnip for meetings, turnip for service, turnip to help one another.

Allow God to Bless us as he has promised He would.

JESUS LOVES ME

Scripture: "I pray that you may have the power . . . to grasp how wide and long and high deep is the love of Christ: Ephesians 3:17-18.

In 1860 Anna B. Warner was asked by her sister Susan to write a song for a Sunday School teacher to sing to a dying boy. Anna wrote one stanza and the chorus of a song that has become one of the most familiar children's hymns of all times. William Bradbury wrote the music in 1862. **Jesus Loves Me.**

A pastor was once heard to say, "I notice that it is always the ***adults*** who choose the children's hymn "**Jesus Love Me"** During hymn sings, it is the adults who sing the loudest because they seem to know it the best."

The Rev. Dr. Jacob Chamberlain, who for many years worked among the Hindus in India, told the story of how he translated the children's hymn into **Telegu,** the native language, and taught it to the children in the day-school. Scarcely a week later as he was going through the narrow streets of the town, he heard singing that sounded familiar. He stopped to listen, and then cautiously drew up to the corner, where he could look down the street. There was a little heathen boy, with heathen men and women standing around him, singing away at the top of his voice: **"Jesus Loves Me this I know."**

As he completed the verse, someone asked the question: "Sonny, where did you learn that song?" "Over at the Missionary School was the answer, "Who is that Jesus, and what is the Bible?" "Oh the Bible is the book from God, they say, to teach us how to get to heaven andJesus is the name of the divine **Redeemer** who came into the world to save us from our sins.

"That is what the missionaries say," "Well, the song is a nice one, come, sing us some more."

And so the boy went on a heathen himself, singing to the heathens about Jesus and his love. That is preaching the gospel by proxy.

A church located in Atlanta was honoring one of its senior pastors. The minister had been retired many years. At age 92, one would wonder why they even bothered to ask him to preach.

After a warm welcome and introduction the old gentleman rose and walked slowly to the pulpit. Without a written paper or notes he began to speak . . .

"When I was asked to come here today and talk to you, your pastor asked me to tell you what was the greatest lesson ever learned in my 50 some years of preaching. I thought about it for three or four days, and I've boiled it down to one thing that made the most difference in my life and has sustained me through all of my trials. The one thing that I could always rely on when tears and heart break came and pain and fear and sorrow paralyzed me. The only thing that would comfort me was this verse . . . . And he began to sing:

"Jesus loves me this I know.
For the Bible tells me so.
Little ones to Him belong,
We are weak but He is strong . . . .
Yes, Jesus loves me . . . .

When he finished, the church was quiet. You could actually hear his footsteps as he shuffled back to his chair. It was an unforgettable moment simplified to its simplest terms.

There have been many additional stanzas written for this song. For those of us who are middle age (or even those almost there) we need to check out the different versions of **Jesus Loves Me.** For Jesus does in fact loves us.

Amen

LABOR FOR THE LORD

This is **Labor Day** weekend. It is a National legal holiday that was established more than 100 years ago. In 1884 in fact. Over the years it has evolved from a purely **labor union celebration** into a general "last fling of summer" festival. Although it is not a religious holiday per se, we can see it as part of our Christian heritage as we recognize the working class of our nation. It also marks the time that many colleges, secondary and elementary school begin classes. A subtle blessing for all mothers who have endured their kids all summer long.

Labor Day is celebrated on the first Monday of September in the USA. Canada has its own Labor Day holiday.

> As a spiritual thought we need to share some scripture that will bring bearing to this weekend holiday. The following scripture has application:
>
> "What does man gain from all of his labor at which he toils under the sun?
>
> Generations come and generations go, but the earth remains forever.
>
> The sun rises and the sun sets, and hurries back to where it rises.
>
> The wind blows to the south and turns to the north, round and round it goes ever returning on its course.
>
> All streams flow into the sea, yet the sea is never full.
>
> To the place the streams come from, there they return again.

All things are wearisome, more than one can say.

The eye never has enough of seeing, nor the ear its fill of hearing.

What has been will be again, what has been done will be done again,

The is nothing new under the sun,

Is there anything of which one can say, **Look! This is something new?**

There is no-remembrance of men of old, and even of those who are yet to come will not be remembered by those who follow."

Ecclesiastes 1:3-11

These words found in Ecclesiastes are thought to have been written by King Solomon with his life largely behind him. He takes stock of the world as he has experienced it, between the horizons of birth and death. The latter horizon beyond which man cannot see. And, in spite of all of King Solomon's wisdom and experience he teaches us that God has ordered all things according to His purposes, and that Man should be patient and enjoy life as God gives it. Man should know his own limitations and not vex himself. He should be prudent in everything, living carefully before God, fearing God and keeping His commandments.

Of course being a Senior Citizen and having experienced various events in our lives we sometimes have a tendency to think that we have all of the answers , . . . and then sometimes we only wished we did. Someone once said, **"Remember, once you get over the hill, you'll begin to pick up speed."**

I heard a cute story the other day and if you will allow me to share it with you I will:
Seems an older couple were lying in bed one morning.
They had just awakened from a good night's sleep.

91

He takes her hand and she responds, "Don't touch me."
"Why not?" He asked.
She answered, "Because I'm dead"

The husband asked, "What are you talking about?"
Were are both lying in bed together, and talking to one another."
She said "No, I'm definitely dead"
He insisted, "You are not dead."

"What in the world makes you think you're dead?"
"Because I woke up this morning and nothing hurts."

Scriptures teach us that God won't give us more than we can handle. But then there are times when we wish that He didn't trust us quite so much.

King Solomon concludes his writings with this passage found in Ecclesiastes 12: 13.

Fear God and keep his commandments, for this is the whole duty of man.
For God will bring every deed into judgment.
Including every hidden thing, whether it is good or evil.

Closing prayer.

THE BRIDGE TO NOWHERE

In November 1998, Hurricane Mitch ravaged the Honduras, Central America. More than 5,600 people perished, 12,500 were injured and 8,600 disappeared. In addition to the loss of human life, 150 bridges were damaged or destroyed. The most modern of all the bridges, *The Choluteca Bridge* survived intact but suffered the greatest indignity, the river moved right out from under it leaving it high and dry and its builders wondering what to do next and how to fix it.

The pictures of the "stand alone bridge" are graphic. Hurricane Mitch poured 100 inches of rain in three days on the area, creating a chain of destruction that resulted in this modern, recently built bridge without access roads, standing alone. The course of the river it spanned was changed by the torrents of water that carved a new river bed minus the bridge. Hence, the "Bridge to Nowhere" now spans dry land.

Perhaps we can draw a parallel between the Bridge and our own Church in East Greenwich.

This church is a stable, thriving church. We are being served by an outstanding "Bridge Minister. We have strong committees and a loving congregation who share a Christian resolve that is our "glue".

"The body is a unit, though it is made up of many parts: and Though all of it parts are many they form one body." 1 Cor. 12:12

But like the **Bridge To Nowhere,** we need to be cognizant of what needs to be done to preserve and enhance the future of the First Baptist Church of East Greenwich. Every part of the church, including but not limited to the Christian Education Department, the Deacons, the Pulpit Supply committee, the Building and Grounds committees, the Board, the Worship Services, the Choir, the Fellowship Dinners, the Youth activities the Outreach and Visitation ministries and so many more all need to remain focused and challenged. In closing, let us not overlook that there may be smaller less obvious bridges that quietly await our outreach. Energy spent on little bridges is energy well spent.

"If one part suffers, every part suffers with it; if one part is Honored, every part rejoices with it," 1 Cor. 12:26

Amen

THE BRIDGE TO NOWHERE

The Choluteca Bridge after the November 1998 Hurricane Mitch

The Church an Organ, a Bell, and a Clock

The word church in the New Testament is *ekklesia,* which means literally the **calling out,** an assembly of a congregation or community. The word church is found only three times in the gospels, Matthew, Mark, Luke and John.

Paul the missionary, founder of many churches, created a famous metaphor that adds to the meaning of **Church.** In Romans 12:5, Paul writes: *"So in Christ we who are many form one body."* The Church. It is not a building or a structure, but rather the act of gathering scattered people into an organic unity in Christ, making a single living organism. Paul had a very strong notion of the Christian community. He believed that the church would develop **love and unity** and that it would grow and attract new members, helping each other and strengthening one another. And so it has.

As you think about **The Church,** perhaps you think about your favorite church. The one that is closest to your heart. Maybe it is local, maybe is it far away. It might be the church that you grew up in. Or the church in which you were baptized. It might be the church in which you were married, or the one in which your children were confirmed, or received their first communion. Such churches hold beloved memories.

One of my favorite Churches is located in Springfield, Illinois. The church in which I was married, the church that my family attended regularly and the church that offered me such wonderful opportunities to be of service.

There is a Church in Washington, D.C. which is a famous historical church. It is the **Calvary Baptist Church** of Washington. It is an old church, built in 1886, famous for it preaching, its great congregations and its affect on the nation's Capital. Its history goes back to the days of Andrew Jackson and Martin Van Buren.

When the congregation was called together to build the church building there was a man by the name of Amos Kendall who was instrumental in raising the monies needed to build the church.

He was a financial advisor to Samuel Morse the inventor of the telegraph and although he never joined the church he gave generously to its growth. But, Amos Kendall had three stipulations:
1. The Church must have an organ.
2. The Church must have a bell, and.
3. The Church must have a pulpit clock.

Each stipulation had a symbolic reference:

The **organ** was a mighty instrument. On it was played thunderous anthems and melodious hymns. With the many keys on the organ console each represented a certain pitch or tone that made harmony and rendered a beautiful message. Let one key not play or get stuck and it might make the tune offensive and unpleasant to the ear. And so the message that we receive is portrayed as keys of the organ, we need to function in harmony and in unity.

The **bell** is another symbol. It was used as a call to worship. First the ringing of the bell was an invitation to come to worship. The second ringing affirmed that the people had assembled and the worship service was to begin.

The bell was also an invitation to get ready for a joyous wedding, a new birth or to memorialize a death in the family. It was often used as a fire alarm calling the volunteers to come and fight the fire. The bell proclaims God's word and rings out the conviction of religious freedom.

Oscar Hammerstein, after being diagnosed with cancer went to Mary Martin's dressing room during the performance of **Sound of Music** and added these words to her famous song:

> "A bell is no bell till you ring it.
> A song is no song till you sing it.
> Love in your heart wasn't put there to stay,
> For love isn't love till you give it away."

Symbolism of the **clock.** I know some preachers who would rather not have to look at a pulpit clock. They want to keep talking. But, the clock reminds us we don't have forever to serve God while in this world. When the moment passes it is gone. We are called to be Christ's representative now and not later. In Frankenmuth, Michigan, a town that has been built to represent a Bavarian Village, there is a large tower clock in the town square. On the hour the clock doors open and outcome carvings of musicians and dancers who dance and swirl as the clock strikes the hour. One day a young girl and her mother were watching . . . . out came the characters, the clock began to strike . . . . 9—10—11—12—but it didn't stop, 13—14—15 . . . and the little girl took her mother's hand and said, **"Mommy is it later than it has ever been before."** And So It Is.

Amos Kendall's stipulations were prophetic. The **organ** does symbolize the harmony and unity that is needed in the Church, in our lives and in our relationships. The **Bell** proclaims peace and love that we receive from God. The **Clock** is a constant reminder that now is the time to be God's servant.

May the gifts and symbols be forever in your hearts and in your minds.

A number of stories and illustrations were taken from a sermon given by Rev. James Miller, East Greenwich, RI 9/07

The Great Pumpkin

Paul writing to the Church of Colossae, in the New Testament Book of **Colossians,** expresses his concern because the young church that had been established by Epaphras and other converts of Paul, had become a target of heretical attacks and had suffered some serious problems in its growth. Paul doesn't go into great detail but he suggests that the heresy was diverse in nature and he makes a number of recommendations. In Colossians 3:2 he writes: *"Set your minds on things above, not on earthy things."*

Ceremonialism was one thing that Paul addressed. **Ceremonialism** held strict rules about the kinds of food and drink, religious festivals and circumcision. Paul says, *"God has chosen to make known among the Gentiles the glorious riches of this mystery, which is Christ in you, the hope of glory. We proclaim him, admonishing and teaching everyone with all wisdom, so that we may present everyone perfect in Christ."* **Colossians 1:27-28**

One festival that we recognize today is **Halloween.** It is one of the oldest holidays with origins going back thousands of years. It has had an influence on many cultures over the centuries.

It is known as **Pomona Day** by the Romans, **Festival of Samhain,** (pronounced sow-in) by the Celtics and the Christians called the holiday **All Saints** or **All Souls Day,** and later changed it to **Hallow Mass,** or **All Hallows.** It was celebrated with big bonfires, parades, people dressed up in costumes like angels and devils and included the carving of gourds, potatoes and squash.

> Pumpkins are fruits, A pumpkin is a type of squash and is a member of the gourd family
>
> (Cucurbitacae) which also includes squash, cucumbers, gherkins and melons.

The largest pumpkin pie ever baked was in 2005 and weighed 2,020 pounds. The largest pumpkin ever grown weighed 1,689 pounds grown by Joe Jutras of North Scituate, RI in September 2007. Pumpkins have been grown in North America for more than 5000 years

Pumpkins are low in calories, fat and sodium and high in fiber. They are a good source of Vitamin A, Vitamin B, potassium and iron. Pumpkin seeds should be planted between the last week in May and the middle of June. They take between 90 and 120 days to grow and are picked in October when they are bright orange in color. Their seeds can be saved to grow new pumpkins next year.

Pumpkin carving is a popular part of the modern American Halloween celebration. They can be found everywhere in the country from doorsteps to dinner tables. Despite the widespread carving that goes on every autumn, few Americans really know why or when the **Jack A Lantern** tradition began

The practice of pumpkin carving originated from an Irish myth about a man nicknamed "Stingy Jack". Stingy Jack invited the devil to have a drink with him. True to his name, Stingy Jack didn't want to pay for the drink so he convinced the Devil to turn himself into a coin that Jack could use to buy their drinks. Once the Devil did so, Jack decided to keep the money and put it into his pocket next to a silver cross which prevented the Devil from changing back into to his original form. Jack eventually freed the Devil under the condition that he would not bother him for one year and should Jack die he would not claim his soul. The next year Jack again tricked the Devil into climbing a tree to pick some fruit. When the Devil was up in the tree Jack carved a sign of the cross in the tree's trunk so that the Devil could not get down until he promised Jack not to bother him for ten more years,

Soon after Jack died., as the legend goes, but God would not allow such an unsavory figure into heaven. The Devil, upset with the tricks Jack had played on him would not allow him into Hell. So, Jack had nowhere to go. The Devil sent Jack off into the dark night with only a burning coal to light his way. Jack put the coal into a carved out turnip and has been roaming the Earth ever since. The Irish began to refer to this ghostly figure as **"Jack of the Lantern"** and then simply **Jack A Lantern".**

In Ireland and Scotland, people began to make their own versions of Jack's lantern carving scary faces in turnips or potatoes and placing them in the windows or near the doors to frighten away Stingy Jack and other evil spirits. In England large beets were used. Immigrants from these countries brought the tradition to the United States and found that pumpkins, native to America, make perfect Jack A Lanterns.

Being a **Christian** is like being a pumpkin. God lifts you up—takes you in and washes all the dirt off of you. He opens you up, touches you deep inside and scoops out all the yucky stuff—including the seeds of doubt—hate—and greed. Then He carves you a new smiling face and puts His light inside you to shine for all the World to see.

Closing prayer.

THE ADVENT CALENDAR

The word **Advent** has a Latin origin . . . . meaning *"the coming."* Or perhaps more accurately,

"coming toward." For Christians, one of the greatest events of the year is the celebration of the birth of our Savior Jesus Christ. We acknowledge this as the greatest gift ever given by God to mankind. Jesus, the son of God, born into this world in human form and coming to live among us to show us the true nature of God, experiencing human joy and sorrow, and finally willing to go to the cross to die for us and pay for all human sins, so that we might have hope of life eternal.

The importance of this event caused many Christians to feel that having only **one day, Christmas,** wasn't enough for celebrating this incredible gift from God. Believers had such a sense of awe and overwhelming gratitude for what had happened that first **Christmas Day,** they felt a need for a period of preparation immediately beforehand. That way, they could take time to meditate on it, and also teach their children the tremendous significance of Christmas.

At first, the days preceding Christmas were marked off from December 1 with chalk on believers' doors. Then, in Germany in the late 19th century, the mother of a child named Gerhard Lang made her son an **Advent Calendar** comprised of 24 tiny sweets stuck on a cardboard. It reminded her son that the greatest celebration of the whole year was approaching. Anticipate it and be grateful.

When Gerhard grew up he went into the printing business and in 1908 he produced what is thought to be the first ever **Advent Calendar,** with small colored pictures for each day in Advent. Later on, he hit on an idea of making the pictures into little shuttered windows for each child to open day by day to heighten their sense of expectation of the coming of Christmas.

The idea of the Advent Calendar caught on and as the demand increased many versions were produced, some had Bible verses pertaining to the Advent period. Unfortunately, the custom came to an end with the beginning of World War I when cardboard was rationed and only allowed to be used for necessary projects. However, in 1946, when rationing began to ease following the end of the Second World War, the tradition once again introduced the colorful little Advent Calendar. It was an instant success.

Sadly today, the Advent Calendar, still enormously popular with children, has lost its true meaning. Many children and their parents have no idea of the history of the little calendar or its true purpose, which is to prepare us for the celebration of the advent of the **Christ-child.** Even if they do know, most don't care. The makers of today's Advent Calendars are anxious only to sell their product, and many don't know or don't care about the meaning and the purpose of **Advent.** The calendars depict Santa Claus and his reindeer, snowmen, holly, mistletoe and all the secular trappings of Christmas, behind the little windows, often along with a piece of chocolate or some candy treat.

Fortunately however, Christian printers are still with us who manufacture calendars for children that unfold the story of the nativity with each window that is opened. We **Christian believers** pray that one day the whole world will be aware of the incredible wonder of the true meaning of **Advent** and **Christmas.**

Too often we under estimate the power of a touch, a radiance of a smile, or the sound of a kind word, a listening ear, an honest compliment, or the smallest act of caring. May **Advent** help you to remember that we **can** make it a **Christmas Day**, any day for those who come into our lives.

> Romans 8:38 *"And we know that in all things God works for the good of those who love Him, who have been called according to His purpose."*

Closing Prayer

It's Beginning To Look Like Christmas

"It's beginning to look **a lot** like Christmas." Isn't that the title of a popular Christmas song?

True, it is beginning to look a lot like Christmas. We have had a fresh coating of snow, the holiday shoppers are in full swing and we are just a few days away from the time that we celebrate the birth of our Lord and Savior, **Jesus Christ. December 25th.**

Christmas is a joyful time of year. Our hearts should be filled with compassion, love and warmth for our friends, families, and fellow man. But sociologists remind us that this is one of the most stressful times of the year. It seems to be a time of more family abuse, marital problems, neglect and personal indignation than at any other time. We are told that even the suicide rate jumps up during the Christmas holidays.

What we must do is put **Christ** back in Christmas. **"He who has not Christ in his heart . . . . will never find it under the tree."**

Things happen for a reason! Perhaps this story will help you understand and share in the true meaning of Christmas: This is a true story:

A brand new pastor and his wife were assigned to their first ministry . . . to reopen a church in suburban Brooklyn. They arrived in early October full of enthusiasm and excitement about their opportunities. When they saw that the church was run down and needed a lot of work, they set a goal to have the building renovated and done in time to have their first service on **Christmas Eve.**

They worked hard, repairing the pews, painting, plastering and making the church ready. On December 18, they were almost finished, ahead of schedule.

Two days later a terrible driving rainstorm hit the area and lasted for two days.

On the 21st the pastor went to the church and his heart sank when he discovered that the roof had leaked and caused a large area of plaster, about **5** feet by **10** feet to fall off the front wall just behind the pulpit.

The pastor cleaned up the mess and not knowing what to do planned to cancel the Christmas Eve service.

On his way home he noticed that a local business was having a flea market sale so he stopped in. One of the items that caught his eye was a beautiful, handmade, ivory colored, crocheted tablecloth. The work was exquisite. It had a Cross embroidered right in the center. It was just the right size to cover up the hole in the front wall. He bought it and headed back to the church.

It had started to snow. An old woman running to catch a bus, missed it and the pastor invited her to wait in the warm church for the next bus that was due in 45 minutes.

She sat in a pew and paid no attention to the pastor while he got a ladder, hangers and tools to put up the tablecloth as a wall **tapestry.** The pastor could hardly believe how beautiful it looked and how it covered the spot on the wall perfectly.

Then he noticed the woman walking down the center aisle. Her face was as white as a sheet. "Pastor," she asked, "Where did you get the tablecloth?" The pastor explained.

The woman asked him to check the lower right corner to see if the initials **EBG** were crocheted there. They were. These were the woman's initials, and she had made this tablecloth **35 years** ago in Austria.

The woman explained that she and her husband had lived in Austria, and were from a well-to-do family. When the Nazis came she was forced to leave. Her husband was going to follow her the next week. But, he was captured and sent to a prison camp and she never saw him again.

The pastor wanted to give her the tablecloth but she made him keep it for the church.

The pastor insisted on driving her home, it was the least that he could do. She lived way over on the other side of Staten Island.

What a wonderful service they had on **Christmas Eve.** The church was nearly full.

The music and the spirit was great. At the end of the service the pastor and his wife greeted everyone at the door and many said they would be back.

One older man stayed in the pew and stared at the front of the church. The pastor wondered why he wasn't leaving. Then the man asked the pastor where he had gotten the tablecloth that was hanging on the front wall, because it was identical to the one that his wife had made many years ago in Austria. **"How could there be two tablecloths so much alike?"** He told of how the Nazis came, how he was arrested and put in prison, and that he had never seen his wife or his home again in 35 years.

The pastor asked if he would allow him to take him for a little ride. They drove to Staten Island and to the same house where the pastor had taken the woman three days earlier. He helped the man climb the three flights of stairs to the woman's apartment, knocked on the door and witnessed the greatest **Christmas** reunion he could imagine.

God works in mysterious ways . . . . Everything is possible for him who believes" Mark 9:23

I ask the Lord to bless you as I pray for you today. To guide you and protect you as you go about your way. His love is always with you, His promises are true, and when you give Him all your cares you know He'll see you through.

Closing prayer.

GROWING OLDER

Some time ago I read about an American man named Arthur Reed who was 123 years old.

The facts about Mr. Reed were astounding. He married for the third time when he was 92, he took 5-mile walks when he was 100. He rode a bicycle until he was 110. He worked until he was 116. When he was asked the secret of his long life, he replied, "**They made me of good dirt.**" Certainly having "good dirt:" helps. Having longevity in your gene pool also helps.

The writer of Psalm 90 suggests that anything beyond **70 years of age** is an exception to the rule. No matter if we are made of "good dirt", our bodies will eventually go the way of the fast fading flowers, the fleeting morning mists, and the dissipating clouds. And in the process we suffer with all of the aches and pains and the curses of old age.

Morris, an 82 year old man, went to the doctor to get a physical. A few days later, the doctor saw Morris walking down the street with a gorgeous young woman on his arm. The Doctor confronted Morris and said, "You're really doing great, aren't you?" Morris replied, "Just doing what you said, Doc: "**Get a hot mama and be cheerful**"

The Doctor gasped, "I didn't say that . . . . I said, You've got a heart murmur" be careful."

Why is it that we always seem to hear what we want to hear and ignore the truth? Maybe that is a trait of growing old.

It seems that mankind has always been searching for the secret to **long life.** Don Juan Ponce DeLeon, the explorer, came to America with Columbus, in 1493, during the second visit to the new world, and was famous for discovering and exploring Florida. It was there that he supposedly discovered the Fountain of Youth. If he had, why did he die when he did? The Psalmist wants us to see how short **our time on earth is . . . . in contrast to eternity.**

A senior citizen said to his eighty-year old buddy:
So I hear you getting married?
Yep!
Do I know her?
Nope.
This woman, is she good looking?
Not really.
Is she a good cook?
Naw, she can't cook too well.
Does she have lots of money?
Nope, poor as a church mouse. Why in the world do you want
to marry her then?
Because she can still drive.

Obviously, this man had his priorities all out of balance. What was important to him was that he needed a way to get around. What he really wanted was a chauffeur, not a wife

Psalm 90:12 says, "*Teach us to number our days that we may gain a heart of wisdom*". Someone once said, "Isn't it a shame that the Lord wastes **Wisdom** on the youth and keeps it for the elderly?"

The psalmist wants to us to be aware of how **short** our time on earth is . . . . **in contrast to eternity.** We should not live our lives assuming that even the longest life gives us plenty of time to prepare for eternity. **Today is the day of salvation!**

Joshua was 40 ears old when Moses sent him to reconnoiter the promise land. Forty five years later Joshua reported "Here I am today, 85 years old. I am still as strong today as I was on the day that Moses sent me. My strength now is as my strength was then." Joshua 14: 10b-11.

Can we boast the same thing? Some of us seem to age quickly, while others wear the years well.

But no matter how we have weathered the years, or for how long—**The Lord has work for us to do.** Even as a senior citizen, like myself, we can serve the Lord at home, at church or in the community. We can set examples of our Christianity among our friends and neighbors and our associates in the rehab center. Remember; "**What we weave in time . . . we will wear in Eternity.**"

Oh, why not turn while still you may,
Too late it soon will be—
A glorious life you can possess
Throughout eternity.

Amen

Ending prayer.

FEBRUARY 29TH . . .
A LEAPING PERSON

In the **Gregorian Calendar,** the standard calendar used in most of the world today, most years that are divisible by **4** are known as **Leap years.** In a **leap year,** the month of February has **29 days** instead of 28. Adding an extra day to the calendar every four years compensates for the fact that a **solar year** is almost 6 hours longer than 365 days

Why is it important to Christians that we have a **Leap year?** The **Gregorian** calendar was designed to keep the vernal equinox on or as close to March 21 as possible so that the date of **Easter** can be celebrated on the **Sunday** after the 14th day of the Moon that falls on or after the 21st of March. **Seasons and astronomical events** do not repeat at the exact number of full days, so a calendar which had the same number of days in each year would over time drift with respect to the events it was supposed to track. By occasionally inserting an additional day into the year the drift can be corrected. A year which is not a **leap year** is called a common year.

Having said all of that, we acknowledge that today is the 29th of February in our **leap year.** Is there anyone here today who celebrates their birthday on the 29th of February? Congratulations! You are unique. If you have celebrated seven birthdays in your life time you are 28 years of age. Ten birthdays would make you 40 years old, and twenty birthdays would mean that you 80 years old. Just think of all the ice cream and cake you have missed over that time.

My wife has a favorite expression when someone asks her how old she is. Her answer is, "**I don't know how old I am, . . . except that I have had 76 birthdays.**" That wouldn't work if she were a **Leaping person,** a person who was born on the 29th of February. She would have to say that she has had only 19 birthdays. Now that might not be so bad after all.

"Blessed are the flexible, for they shall not be bent out of shape."

Psalms 42:11 reads, 'WHY ART THOU CAST DOWN, O MY SOUL? HOPE THOU IN GOD."

A friend of mine, who was a **Leap year** baby, seemed to always struggle with the fact that she was never able to have the kind of birthday celebration that others had. She was feeling down in the dumps one Sunday and admitted that she was having a birthday that day, February 29, and things weren't lining up to make it much of a celebration. She hadn't received any phone calls or cards and the only gift she had received was one of those practical ones for which husbands are famous and wives don't appreciate. Something like a new chrome-plated tire iron. Her hints about going out to eat had fallen on deaf ears and a. birthday cake seemed out of the question.

The highlight of the day would be at church where the pastor always asked the congregation to sing **"Happy Birthday"** to anyone whose birthday fell on Sunday.

She said that she waited expectantly through the announcements, waited through the opening hymn, waited while the pastor mentioned another birthday coming up during the week. And then he began his sermon.

How could he be so forgetful? She felt slighted, overlooked, disappointed. Why do people take me for granted, Lord? Especially today of all days?

A few minutes later, an old hymn, **"Be Thou My Vision."** redirected her focus. Two lines in particular spoke directly to her soul. *"Riches I need not, nor man's empty praise, Thou mine inheritance, now and always."* How could she have been so forgetful as to overlook God's blessings during the past year and throughout her lifetime?

Don't we often feel like my friend? We feel as though the world has passed us by and no one really cares. But, we need to refocus and praise the Lord for all that He has done for us.

We thank you Lord that the up side of down times is that You use them to put things into their proper perspective.

We don' always remember days . . . . but rather moments. Life moves too fast . . . . so enjoy your precious moments. God is good.

The Lord will reward everyone for whatever good he does . . . . Ephesians 6:8

Closing prayer.

WHY IS THE RESURRECTION OF JESUS IMPORTANT?

Today, when I awoke, I realized that this was the **best day** of my life, **ever.** There were times when I wondered if I would make it to today, but I did. And because I did, I'm going to **celebrate.** Today I'm going to celebrate what an unbelievable life I have had so far. The many blessings, and yes, the hardships, because they have served to make me stronger. And I marvel at God's seemingly simple gifts that continue to come to me through Him.

Recently I learned of a young four year old boy, whose next door neighbor was an elderly man who had just lost his wife. Upon seeing the gentleman sitting on his porch, sadly looking out at his backyard, the boy went to the old man, climbed up in his lap and just sat there.

When his mother asked him what he had said to the neighbor, the little boy just said, "Nothing, I just helped him cry."

Easter is the day when the world celebrates the resurrection of Jesus Christ. In **325 AD** the Council of Nicea ruled that Easter should be celebrated on the first **Sunday** after the full moon following the eternal equinox. The date of Easter varies between the 22nd of March and the 25th of April. This year we will celebrate **Easter** on April 8, 2007. The Christian Church celebrates the resurrection each Lord's Day

Jesus was crucified on **Friday.** We refer to it as **Good Friday,** because it was a good day for mankind. Jesus died for us that we may have forgiveness of sin. **John 19: 17-18** describes the event: *"He was taken out of the city, he carried his own cross, he went out to the place of the Skull. Here they crucified him, and with him two others, one on each side and Jesus in the middle."*

Crucifixtion was a horrible death. The agony of the victim was horrific because it brought about so much pain. The pain of nailing the victim to the cross; the suffering caused by the abnormal position of the body, arms outstretched with body weight pulling down; and the traumatic fever induced by hanging for a long period of time was excruciating. Jesus suffered.

In the book of Mark we read the account of Jesus' death. *"At the sixth hour darkness came over the whole land until the ninth hour. And at the ninth hour Jesus cried out in a loud voice "Eloi, Eloi, lama sabachthani', which means,*

> *'My God, my God, why have you forsaken me?* versus 37 concludes,
> *"With a loud cry Jesus breathed his last breath"* **Mark 15: 33-34, 37.**

Since this was the day before the Sabbath, and evening approached, there was an urgency to get Jesus' body down from the cross before sundown, when the Sabbath began. Joseph of Arimathea asked Pilate for the body and Pilate gave his permission. Joseph brought some linen cloth, took down the body and wrapped it in linen, and placed it is a tomb cut out of rock. He placed a stone against the entrance of the tomb in order to seal it.

On the third day, when the Sabbath was over, Mary Magdalene, and Mary, mother of James, brought spices so that they might anoint Jesus' body. Very early on the first day of the week, Sunday, just after sunrise they went to the tomb and found it empty. **Jesus had arisen!**

Now for the question: **WHY IS THE RESURRECTION OF JESUS IMPORTANT?**

It is important for several reasons.
1. It witnesses to the **immense power** of God himself. To believe in the Resurrection is to believe in God. If God exists, and if He created the Universe and has power over it, He has power to raise the dead. If **not** He isn't a God worthy of our faith and worship.

Only He who **created** life can resurrect it after death.
Only He can **reverse** the hideousness that is death itself.
Only He can **remove** the sting that is death.
God reminds us of His **absolute sovereignty** over life and death.

2. The resurrection of Jesus is a testimony to the resurrection of human beings which is a basic tenet of the Christian faith. Christianity alone possesses a founder who transcends death and who promises that His followers will do the same. All other religions are founded by men and prophets who have ended up in the grave.

As Christians we take comfort in the fact that our God **became man**, **died for our sins**, was crucified, dead and buried, and **arose** on the third day, as was promised in the scriptures. The grave could not hold Him. He **lives** and He sits at the right hand of God, the Father in Heaven. **The Living Church Has a Living Head.**

In 1 Corinthians 15 Paul explains in detail the importance of the resurrection of Christ.

In this chapter he gives six disastrous consequences if there was **not** a resurrection:
1. **Preaching** Christ would be senseless
2. **Faith** in Christ would be useless.
3. **All witnesses** would be liars.
4. **No one** would be redeemed from sin.
5. **All former believers** would have perished.
6. **Christians** would be the most pitied people on earth.

The inspired **Word of God** guarantees our resurrection and the return of Jesus at the **Rapture.**
The Resurrection is the triumphant and glorious victory for every believer in Jesus Christ.
It proves that God has the power to raise us from the dead. It guarantees that those who believe in Christ will not remain dead, but will be resurrected into eternal life. That is our blessed hope.

Closing prayer

God Opposes The Proud But Gives Grace To The Humble

When my children were young we spent a lot of time discussing questions they had about God, Heaven, Angels and many other religious subjects. Oh yes, we can't forget the Devil because he is always there. We talked about the Devil too.

One great truth came out of one of our discussions, and that was, **"No matter hard you try, you can't baptize cats."**

During one of our discussions my oldest son asked, **"If everything comes from God, and He gives us everything that we ask for, then how come we don't have everything?"**

The answer is: **God doesn't give us everything we ask for. He gives us everything we need, when we need it.**

James, the brother of Jesus, writes to the twelve tribes of the Jewish nation.

The book of James is thought to be one of the earliest letters in the New Testament. James was called the pillar of the church by Paul.

In James 4: we read: *"You **want** something but you don't get it . . . . You kill, you covet. But you can't have what you want. You quarrel and fight. You do not have because you do not ask God. When you ask, you do not receive because you ask with the wrong motive.*

And so it is

As James says, sometimes we ask for the wrong thing. We want things that will hurt us **A big thick chocolate malted milk shake.** Hum that sounds delicious. But God know that will hurt me so He doesn't give me that. God gives us things because He loves us.

God, wants to give us what is good for us.

Another question that was always asked, **"Why didn't I get what I prayed for?"**

There are three types of persons when it comes to prayer:

1. Those who don't ask.
2. Those who ask with the wrong motives
3. Those who consider what God wants and prays accordingly.

A Sunday School teacher asked her fourth grade students to write a letter to God and ask for something they wanted. Here are a few of the letters:

Dear God: I'll bet it is hard for you to love everybody in the whole World There are only four people in my family and we fight all the time. Nancy

Dear God: Maybe Cain and Abel wouldn't kill each other so much if they had their own rooms. It works with me and my brother. Larry.

Dear God: Thank you for my baby brother, but what I prayed for was a puppy. Joyce

Dear God: Please send Dennis Clark to a different camp this summer. Peter

Dear God: I think about you all the time, sometimes even when I am not praying. Elliot

Dear God: If you will watch in church on Sunday I will show you my new shoes. Mickey

Dear God: If we come back as something else, please don't let me be Jennifer Horton, I hate her. Denise

Someone once said, "Be careful what you pray for, you might get it."

James summarizes it very succinctly in verse 4:6 "**God opposes the proud but gives grace to the humble.**"

> *"Submit yourselves then to God. Resist the Devil and he will flee from you.*
> *Come near to God and He will come near to you."*

Amen

THE LENTEN LESSON

Many Christians wonder about the traditions and events leading up to **Easter.** We learn of the events that tell **of the crucifixion of Jesus Christ,** but if we go to the scriptures and try to find details we may not find a great deal of information on the various days of Lent. Of course we can find accounts of the **Last Supper** in the four Gospels, **Matthew, Mark, Luke and John.** But we would find little about **Shrove Tuesday, Ash Wednesday, Laetare Sunday, Maundy Thursday, and Good Friday.**

The Bible contains numerous accounts of people using "dust and ashes" as a symbol of repentance and mourning. One example is Daniel, God's prophet who said:

> **"Then I turned to the Lord and prayed and ask Him**
> **For help. I did not eat any food. To show my sadness**
> **I put on rough cloth and sat in ashes. I prayed to the Lord**
> **my God and told him about all of my sins." Daniel 9:3**

At the beginning of the 11th century it became a custom in the church for all of the faithful to take part in **a** ceremony on the Wednesday, known as Ash Wednesday. In the Christian calendar, we find a day known as **Shrove Tuesday.** This is the day before **Ash Wednesday.** It is also known as **Pancake Day.** The name Shrove comes from the English verb **shrive** which means "To absolve people of their sins." It is another way of using up the milk and eggs and flour prior to **Lent.**

Lent begins with Ash Wednesday. There are 40 days between Lent and **Easter.** Traditionally, during this time Christians observe the period by fasting, avoiding festivities, and performing acts of penance. Meat, fish eggs and milk products were strictly forbidden and only one meal a day was eaten. Making the sign of the cross in ashes on a person's forehead was a symbol of that person's identification with Jesus Christ.

Ash Wednesday is not a *holy day of obligation* for many congregations, but many people would not think of letting Ash Wednesday go by without a trip to church to be marked with ashes on their forehead. Since the Bible doesn't command or condemn the procedure, a Christian is at liberty to prayerfully decide to observe Ash Wednesday, or not. If you feel led to the Lord to observe Ash Wednesday and Lent, the important thing is to have a Biblical perspective. It is good to repent of sinful ways. It is also good to identify yourself as a Christian. But, we should never believe that God will automatically bless us in response to the observing of a ritual.

God is interested in our hearts, not in our doing rituals. Remember, God loves us because of who God is, not because of anything we have or have not done.

> Three things in life that once they are gone never come back: **Time, Word, Opportunity.**
> Three things in life that are never certain: **Fortune, Success, Dreams.**
> Three things that make a person significant: **Commitment, Sincerity, Hard work.**

Laetare Sunday is the fourth Sunday in Lent, marking the half way point of Lent.

The Sunday before Easter is the beginning of Holy Week and we know that is the day that Jesus made his triumphal entry into Jerusalem, passing through the **Golden** Gate. As prophesied, he entered riding on a young colt and the people greeted him with palm branches. We know it as **Palm Sunday** The people expected the messiah to become their new King and free them from the Roman bondage. While Jesus was in Jerusalem he cleaned the temple, and cursed the fig tree. He was anointed and learns of a sinister plot that would send him to the cross.

On Thursday of that week Jesus met with his disciples in the **Upper Room** for the Passover dinner. Jesus established the **Lord's Supper** as recorded in Matthew 26: 17-29. This day is known as **Maundy Thursday. Christians celebrate Jesus by taking communion. Mark 14: 21-25**

Good Friday is a holy day shared by Christians on the Friday before Easter. It preserves the memory of the pain and suffering at the crucifixion of Jesus. He was treated like a criminal, purged and beaten, mocked and rejected by the people. He was hung on the cross, and he died for our sins.

It was the day Jesus Christ gave his life for remission of sin, and gave us the promise of eternal life.

"Whoever believes and is baptized will be saved, but whoever does not believe will be condemned."
Mark 16:16

Easter is the day that we celebrate the resurrection. As prophesied, Jesus arouse from the grave and proved that he is the Son of God He defeated death that we might have hope of eternal life.

Closing Prayer

THE WISE OLD MAN'S STORY

A man of 92 years, tall, lean, well presented, who obviously took great care of his appearance, was moving into an old folks home. His wife of 65years had recently died and he was obliged to leave his home for a place that could give him additional care and attention.

After waiting several hours in the retirement home lobby, he gently smiled as he was told that his room was ready.

As he slowly walked to the elevator, using his cane, an attendant described his small room to him. It included a sheet that hung in the window which served as a curtain, it has . . . The old man interrupted, "I like it very much," he said with the enthusiasm of an 8 year old boy who had just been given a new puppy.

"But sir, you haven't even seen the room yet, we are almost there," said the attendant.

"That has nothing to do with it," he replied, **"I am happy with it."**

"Happiness is something that I choose in advance. Whether or not I like the room doesn't depend on the furniture, or the decor—rather it depends on **how I decide to see it**. It is already decided in my mind that I like my room. It is a decision I make every morning when I wake up."

"I can choose to spend my day in bed . . . . enumerating all the difficulties that I have with the parts of my body that no longer work very well, or I can get up and give thanks to God for those parts that are still in working order. And so it is."

"Every day is a gift and as long as I can open my eyes I will focus on the new day and all of the happy memories that I have had during my life time."

"Old age is like a **bank account**. You withdraw in later life what you have deposited along the way." So my advice to you is to deposit all the happiness you can in your **bank account of memories.** Then you can recall them as you need them."

Thank you for your part in filling my bank account with happy memories, which I am still continuing to fill each blessed day.

Remember these simple guidelines for happiness:

1. **Free your heart from hate.**
2. **Free your mind from worry.**
3. **Live simply.**
4. **Give more, and**
5. **Expect less.**

As We Approach
Easter Sunday

Many Christians wonder about the traditions and customs of worship events leading up to Easter. We all have learned about how Jesus was crucified in Jerusalem after He was condemned by Pontius Pilate. How the people seemed to turn against him and how he died on a wooden cross at Calvary, a hill called Golgotha. Golgotha means "The place of the skull."

The crucifixion of Jesus full-fills prophecy. God and Jesus knew exactly what had to be done and it was done. However, a number of things happened leading up to this time. Through the ages the church has established a number of "holy days", and events that lead us to that fateful day in Jerusalem.

In the 11th century there was custom started by the church for all of the faithful to take part in a ceremony that we know as Ash Wednesday. This a time 40 days before Easter and is known as the beginning of Lent. During this time Christians observed the period by fasting, avoiding festivities, and performing acts of penance. Meat, fish, eggs, and milk products were strictly forbidden and only one meal a day was eaten. The making of a sign of the cross on a person's forehead was a symbol that the person identified with Jesus Christ.

Ash Wednesday was February 17th this year. It is not a high holy day or a day of obligation, but many Christian Church goers would not think of letting Ash Wednesday go by without a trip to church to be marked with the ashes. Since the Bible doesn't command or condemn the procedure a believer is at liberty to prayerfully decide to observe this day if they wish. The important thing is to have a Biblical perspective. It is always good to repent of sinful ways, and it is good to identify yourself as a Christian. However, we should never believe that God will automatically bless us in response to observing a ritual. ***God is interested in our hearts, not in our rituals. Remember, God loves us because of who God is . . . . not because of anything we have or have not done***

- Three things in life that once they are gone never come back . . . .

Time, words, and opportunity.

- Three things in life are never certain . . . .

Fortune, Success, and dreams

- Three things that make a person significant . . . .

Commitments, Sincerity, and hard work.

The Sunday before Easter is Palm Sunday. This year it is March 28th. It marks the beginning of **Holy Week.** We know Palm Sunday was the day that Jesus made a triumphal entry into Jerusalem through the Golden Gate. The account was beautifully described by Matthew in Chapter 20: 17-19. *"While Jesus was going up to Jerusalem, he took the twelve disciples aside by themselves, and said to them on the way, 'See we are going up to Jerusalem and the Son of Man will be handed over to the chief priests and scribes and they will condemn him to death; they will hand him over to the Gentiles to be mocked and flogged and crucified; and on the third day he will be raised."*

And, as prophesied, he entered the city riding on a young colt. The people greeted Him with palm branches for they expected a new king, a messiah who would free them from the Roman bondage.

While Jesus was in the city he went to the temple and drove out the money lenders and merchants. He cursed the fig tree. He was anointed and he learned more of the sinister plot to send him to the cross. On Thursday of that week he instructed his disciples to prepare the Passover Meal They met in a place known as the Upper Room. It was here that Jesus instituted the **Lord's Supper.**

Matthew 26:26 tells us: *"While they were eating Jesus took a loaf of bread, and after blessing it he broke it, gave it to his disciples and said, 'Take, eat, this is my body.' Then he took the cup and after giving thanks he gave it to them, saying, 'Drink from it all of you; for this is my blood of the covenant, which is poured out for many for the forgiveness of sins. I tell you I will never again drink of this fruit of the vine until that day when I drink it new with you in my Father's kingdom.'* When they had sung a hymn they went out to the Mount of Olives. Then the **betrayal.** Judas, one of Jesus' disciples, had sold out for 30 pieces of silver. The soldiers came and with a kiss from Judas the Son of Man was arrested and taken into custody. Jesus was taken before the high court and Caiaphas, the high priest began the inquiry. The charge was blasphemy, giving false witness. The court decided to find him guilty and condemned him to death.

The next morning Jesus was taken to the Governor, Pontius Pilate. Pilate was a politician. He wanted peace in the territory at any price. After a number of questions, that Jesus refused to answer, Pilate washed his hands of the matter and turned Jesus over to the people to crucify him.

Jesus was beaten and flogged and made to carry his cross up the hill to Calvary. And along side two other criminals he was hung on the cross. From noon until three in the afternoon darkness came over the land. And Jesus was heard to say "Eli, Eli le-ma sa—bach-tha-ni. "My God, My God, why have you forsaken me? Then the curtains of the temple were torn in two, the earth shook and rocks were spit as Jesus took his final breath.

Because the Sabbath law required the body be taken down from the cross and be buried before sunset a rich man by the name of Arimathea volunteered his tomb for internment. The government appointed guards to standby the tomb to secure its entrance.

On Sunday, the first day of the week, Mary Magdalene and the other Mary went to the tomb but before they arrived an earthquake occurred and the stone was rolled away. When they looked into the tomb expecting to see Jesus' body they found the tomb was empty. Jesus had risen as he said he would. Praise the Lord.

Prayer

THE WINDOWS THROUGH
WHICH WE LOOK

Growing up in Springfield, the capital of Illinois, in the heart of Lincoln land,. brings back many wonderful memories of my youth. One of the things I liked to do was ride by and look at a house that was designed by world famous architect, **Frank Lloyd Wright.**

The windows were beautiful and it almost made you want to stop and go in and tour the home. Mr. Wright had used an enormous amount of colorful stained glass in his design and it was intriguing.

Then I remembered an old aphorism, *"People who live in glass houses should never throw stones."* You know what an aphorism is . . . "It is a short pointed sentence expressing a wise or clever observation." Windows are great, we can see in—and the folks who are inside can see out. But windows also need washing, and that is another sermon for another time.

The Windows Through Which We Look, is the title of a story of an interesting young couple who had moved into a new house in a new neighborhood. It was the house of their dreams. The kitchen was located at the rear and it had a beautiful picture window over-looking the backyard. The landscaping was inspiring. They were thrilled and proud to be able to live in this setting.

The first morning, the couple. Sarah and Bill. were eating breakfast and looking out of their picture window when they noticed a young woman who lived next door hanging her wash outside.

"Hmm" said Sarah, "That laundry is not very clean. She probably doesn't know how to wash correctly. Maybe she needs a better laundry soap."

Bill, her husband, looked out, but remained silent. Every time Sarah's neighbor hung her wash out to dry, Sarah would make the same comment. About a month went by when one day Sarah noticed her neighbor had a nice clean wash. She was very surprised.

She said to her husband, "Look Bill, our neighbor has learned how to wash correctly. I wonder who taught her? Maybe she has a new washing machine."

The husband said—" No! I have to tell you this—**I got up early this morning and washed our window."**

And so it is with life—what we see when watching others depends on the PURITY of the window through which we look.

Sometimes we see only what we want to see. Sometimes we let our imaginations get the best of our view. Sometimes our view is clouded and distorted for some reason or another. What we see depends on the purity of the window through which we look.

In Philippians, 4:8 we find these words:

> *. . . fix your thoughts on what is True and Good and Right. Think about things that are Pure and Lovely and dwell on the Fine and Good Things in others. Think about all you can praise God for and be glad about it.*

Remember: :**The nicest thing about the future is that it always starts tomorrow.**

Prayer

WHAT MAKES GOOD FRIDAY GOOD?

Good Friday is a celebration of passion, suffering and death by crucifixion of Jesus Christ.

Several years ago, when my youngest son was about six years of age, the family was preparing to attend a **Good Friday** service at our Church. In a child like innocence, he asked me a very profound question. He said, "Why do we call it Good Friday when that was the day they killed Jesus?"

The day that Jesus died is called **Good Friday** because it was a good day for mankind. Jesus died for us, died in our place, that we may have forgiveness of **sin.** The day was both a sad day and a happy day.

It was sad because Jesus, at the age of 33, was condemned to death. He would die on a cross. Crucifixion was the "worst" possible way to die. It was usually reserved for the most dreadful criminals. Jesus was to be nailed to the cross by his hands and his feet. Each nail was six to eight inches long. The nails were driven into his wrists and his feet. Both feet were nailed together which forced him to support himself on a single nail. Jesus could not support himself with his legs because of the pain so he was forced to alternate between arching his back then using his legs just to continue to breath. Imagine the struggle, the pain, the suffering the courage. Jesus endured this reality for over three hours.

Crucifixion was a horrible event. The agony of the crucified victim was brought about by a number of factors;

(1) The painful character of the wounds inflicted by nailing the victim to the cross.

(2) The suffering caused by the abnormal position of the body; arms outstretched with the weight pulling down and no physical way to get relief.

(3) The traumatic fever induced by hanging for a long period of time in that position

Blood sinks rapidly into the lower extremities of the body and within 6 to 12 minutes blood pressure drops to less than 50%. The heart is deprived of blood which ultimately results in heart failure. However, death by crucifixion did not generally happen for two to three days. As an act of compassion death was often hastened by breaking the victims legs which induced further shock and trauma.

With Jesus, the soldiers saw that he was already dead so they didn't break his legs. *(John 19:33)*

"But when they came to Jesus and saw that he was already dead, they did not break his legs." Instead a Roman soldier pierced his side with a spear. Only water poured from his wound. These things occurred so that the scriptures might be fulfilled.

After these things, Joseph of Arimathea, one of Jesus' disciples, asked Pilate for permission to take the body away and he buried it in a new tomb in the garden in which he died.

It was a sad day because Jesus had suffered and died on the cross. It was a **Happy Day** because Jesus paid the penalty for **our sins.**

At the time, the day did not seem so good. But on Easter morning, after Jesus had arisen from the dead, everyone knew it was **Good.** Because of the passion of Christ, the result is salvation for sinners and therefore the day is known as Good Friday.

Easter is the day on which the Church celebrates the resurrection of Jesus Christ. In 325 AD the Council of Nices ruled that Easter should be the first Sunday after the full moon, following the vernal equinox. That being the time of year, in the spring, when there is equal hours of daylight and darkness. The date for Easter varies from the 22nd of March to the 25th of April.

Furthermore, Christians celebrate the divinity of Jesus by taking communion together as they meet to worship. In **Matthew 26: 26-29** we find scripture that tells of the institution of the Lord's Supper. Jesus had instructed the apostles to go to the upper room in Jerusalem to engage in the Passover Feast. It was the day before Good Friday. It was there that we read this account:

"While they were eating, Jesus took the loaf of bread, and after blessing it he broke it, gave it to the disciples, and said, 'Take eat; this is my body.' Then he took a cup, and after giving thanks he gave it to them saying, 'Drink from it all of you for this is my blood of the covenant, which is poured out for many for the forgiveness of sins.

I tell you I will never again drink of the fruit of the vine until that day when I drink it new with you in my Father's kingdom."

After they had sung a hymn, they went out to the Mount of Olives . . . . It was there that the act of betrayal, the arrest of Jesus by the soldiers, the mockery of a trial before Caiaphas, the high priest, and the hearing before Pontius Pilate, the Governor took place. Pilate, wanting to keep peace at any price, turned Jesus over to the people and "washed his hands" of the whole thing. The people cried, "**Crucify Him**."

Communion.

MEMORIAL DAY REFLECTIONS

Memorial Day 2010 will be celebrated on Monday May 31, this year. As a personal observation I believe that the country seems to be more aware of Memorial Day this year and will participate in it more passionately than in Memorial Days before.

Perhaps the War in Iraq and in Afghanistan has made us more cognizant. We are a peaceful Christian nation that finds itself embroiled in a war that seems to have no end, and yet, we know that it is essential that we fight for that which is right and what we believe is the will of God. "One nation under God, indivisible, with liberty and justice for all".

The price of gasoline has reached $4.00 or more a gallon, and seemly will go higher. We worry about the cost of electricity and heating oil and if we will be able to afford to heat our homes this winter. The housing market is depressed. Unemployment looms over the horizon for many workers. The cost of living continues to rise every time we go to the super market. It seems like we face a crisis every time we turn around. The Bible has some good advice Our resolve is found in the scriptures.

> "I lift up my eyes to the hills, from where does my help come?
> My help comes from the Lord who made heaven and earth.
>
> He will not let your foot be moved. He who keeps you will not slumber.
> Behold he who keeps Israel will neither slumber nor sleep.
>
> The Lord is your keeper. The Lord is your shade on your right hand.
> The sun shall not strike you by day nor the moon by night.
>
> The Lord will keep you from all evil, He will keep your life.
> The Lord will keep you going out and coming in from this time forth and forevermore." Psalm 121

When we face the problems of this world and become anxious about our lives and the lives of our loved ones we need to read **Matthew 6: 25-34:**

> ".... do not be anxious about your life, what you will eat or what you will drink nor about your body, what you will put on. Is not life more than food and body more than clothing? Look at the birds of the air, they neither sow or reap nor gather into barns and yet your heavenly Father feeds them. Are you not of more value than they? And which of you by being anxious can add a single hour to your life?"

> "Therefore, do not be anxious about tomorrow for tomorrow will be anxious for itself."

We need to keep **the solemn and sacred spirit of Memorial Day forever in our hearts and minds.** We need to make it our traditional day of observance. This is the day that we honor our fallen heroes.

Our fathers, our brothers, our sons and our daughters. It must be the day that we praise God and thank him for granting us freedom, and praise those who have sacrificed so much to preserve it.

One tradition that we have is the selling of poppy flowers by members of the Veterans of Foreign Wars.

Traditionally we need to acknowledge and praise God for having allowed us the freedom that we enjoy.

Psalm 119: 45-48 explains: "I will walk in freedom for I have sought out your precepts.

I will speak of your statutes before Kings and not be put to shame. for I delight in your commands because I love them.

I lift up my hands to your commands, which I love and I meditate on your decrees."

Having said that, I would like to tell you a story about a wonderful **"Secret Herb."**

It bothered Ben each time he went to the kitchen and saw the little metal container sitting on the shelf above Martha's cook stove. He probably would not have noticed it so much or had been so curious expect Martha had repeatedly told him never to touch it.

The reason she said was because it contained a "secret herb" from her mother and since she had no way of every refilling it she was concerned that Ben or someone would pick it up and look inside and accidentally drop it spilling its valuable contents.

The container wasn't much to look at. It was old and much of the original red and gold floral colors had faded. But it was obvious that it had received a lot of use by Martha, her mother and her grand-mother.

Martha never cooked without it. She would cook a dish and take the container off the shelf and sprinkle a little of the "secret herb" over the ingredients. Even when she baked cakes, pies or cookies she would add a light sprinkling before she put the pan in the oven.

Whatever was in the container sure worked because Ben felt that Martha was the best cook in the world, and anyone who came to eat at their house shared that opinion. Somehow Martha had stretched the contents over 30 years of marriage. It never failed to effect mouth watering results.

One day Martha became ill and Ben took her to the hospital where she stayed overnight.

When Ben returned home he found the house extremely lonely. He wandered into the kitchen to see what was in the 'frigid" and his eye caught the container on the shelf above the stove.

Curiosity nagged him. What was in the container, and why wasn't he suppose to touch it?

He could not contain himself any lsonger. He carefully took the container off the self and set it on the counter. He pried off the lid and looked inside. The container was empty except for a little folded slip of paper on the bottom. He slowly unfolded it under the kitchen light.

A brief note was scrawled inside, and the handwriting was unmistakably Martha's mothers.

It very simply said, **"Martha—To everything you make, add a dash of LOVE."**

Now Ben understood why Martha's cooking tasted so good.

HOW SHOULD WE THEN LIVE?

The late Christian thinker and writer, **Francis Schaeffer** wrote a book entitled, *"How Should We Then Live?"* He wrote, "In the face of modern secularism, humanism, materialism, and relativism, there seems to be no absolute standards of conduct. In fact, there seems to be a growing lack of civility and respect for God and others. We seem to be living in a world of exploding knowledge, yet more and more people act without **wisdom."** **And so it is.**

"Who is wise?" Remember the **Honeymooners**? Ralph Cramden the character played by Jackie Gleason on that old TV series the Honeymooners? Ralph used to accuse his wife Alice of being a **Wisenheimer** when she refused to support his hair-brained schemes. Maybe we have been guilty of that as well. There is an old axiom that says, *"The longer I live, the more I learn about less and less until someday I'm going to know everything about nothing."*

The Bible Proverbs are full of capsules of truth and wisdom that have stood the test of time. They were written in a culture where reflection of life was a vocation and not just a **"Time-out"** from rapid fire living. They are often the result of keen observations of life. For example: Solomon shows the negative consequences of laziness in Proverbs 24: 30-34.

"I went past the field of the sluggard, past the vineyard of the man who lacks Judgment. Thorns had come up everywhere, the ground was covered with Weeds, and the stone wall was in ruins. I applied my heart to what I observed and learned a lesson from what I saw. A little sleep, a little slumber, a little folding of the hands to rest and Poverty will come to you like a bandit, and scarcity like an armed man."

I am certain that we have all said something at some time that we wished we hadn't said. The answer is found in Proverbs 15:28 . . . . *"The heart of the righteous weighs its answer, but the mouth of the wicked gushes evil."*

Despite the agricultural settings of the times, Proverbs provides us with some moral and ethical principles that are just and relevant, and pertinent to us in our modern, computerized, high-tech life of the 21st century.

Wisdom . . . What is it? According to the Bible it is not only the best course of action or behavior in a given situation but it also involves the right relationship with the Lord and our fellow man. It is a quality which knows and carries out the right responses to certain situations that might leave the unwise uneasy.

Experience can be a great teacher, perhaps the best instructor in life because it reinforces the moral principles that under gird true wisdom. It teaches us that wisdom lies in acknowledging that we do not have all of the answers, thus we must place our lives in the hands of the one who does.

We are told, *"Trust in the Lord with all Thine heart, and lean not unto Thine own understanding,"* Prov. 3:5

Experience can teach us the hazards of disobeying the Laws of God, whether in marriage, personal relationships, respect for others, personal diligence or any other realm of life. One needs to learn this wisdom, so that we can avoid experimenting with evil and thus experiencing for ourselves the disastrous consequences. The reason a bear doesn't tangle with a skunk is not because the giant beast could not disposed of the small animal with one swipe of his paw, but because he knows the consequences of his victory would not be worth the price.

Consequences of evil acts are **"chickens that come home to roost."**

> Scripture says,
> "Be sure your sins will find you out." Numbers 32:23
> "They have sown the wind and they shall reap the whirlwind."
> Hosea 8:7
> "Whatsoever a man soweth, that shall he also reap." Galatians 6:7

Our lack of civility and respect for others and our boorish behavior have already had an effect on our society. Experience is reminding us daily that the path of obedience to God, though sometimes difficult, is always worth the effort.

Proverbs contains so many relevant and practical lessons. Consider these words when rearing a family: **"Train up a child in the way he should go and when he is old he will not depart from it." Prov. 22:6**

How much better off we would be if the members of our society hated the same things that God hates:

Found in Prov., 6:16-19

1. A proud look (haughty eyes)
2. A lying tongue.
3. Hands that shed innocent blood.
4. A heart that devises wicked schemes.
5. Feet that are quick to rush into evil.
6. A false witness who pours out lies.
7. A man who stirs up dissention among brothers.

Wisdom is built on a right relationship with Almighty God, and from it flows the right relationship with our fellow man. Actions that reflect true wisdom may be costly, but in the long run they are always worth the commitment.

Story:

> A man took his car to a garage and told the mechanic, who was a big burly man, that the front end seemed to be out of alignment. The mechanic looked at the car, grabbed a huge hammer and proceeded to beat on part of the right axle.
>
> He road tested the car and he found the problem had been fixed. When the owner looked at the bill for $100 he complained that it was too high. He asked, "How could you charge such an amount for a few strikes with a hammer?"
>
> The mechanic replied, "I'm charging you $5 for the work that was done, and $95 for knowing where to hit."
>
> Doesn't this illustrate the value of **wisdom?** Wisdom that benefits us is sometimes costly. The same is true in our relationship with God. It costs to live by the principle, **"Fear God and keep His Commandments."**
>
> But it costs a great deal more if we don't.

Prayer.

MEMORIAL DAY CELEBRATION

Memorial Day was originally called **Decoration Day**. It is a day of remembrance for those who have died in our nation's service. There are many stories as to its actual beginnings, with over two dozen towns and cities claiming to be the birth place of **Memorial Day.**

There is evidence that there was an organized group of women from the South that were decorating graves before the end of the Civil War. A hymn written in **1867** entitled *"Kneel Where Our Loves are Sleeping"* by Nella L. Sweet, credits the ladies of the South for decorating the graves of the Confederate dead.

Memorial Day was officially proclaimed on May 5, 1868 by General John Logan, National Commander of the Grand Army of the Republic. General Logan's *General Order No. 11* was first observed on May 30, 1868 by placing flowers on the graves of both Union and Confederate soldiers at Arlington National Cemetery.

The first **State** to officially recognize the holiday was New York, in 1873. By 1890 it was recognized by all of the Northern states. The South states refused to acknowledge the day and honored their dead on separate days until after World War I (when the holiday changed from honoring those who died fighting in the Civil War to honoring all **Americans** who died fighting in any war).

Memorial Day is now celebrated by almost every State on the last Monday in May. A bill was enacted by Congress in 1971 that made it a three day weekend and a Federal Holiday.

In 1915, inspired by a poem, *"In Flanders Fields"*, by **John McCrae, Moina Michael,** wrote this verse:

> "We cherish too. The Poppy red.
> That grows on fields where valor led,
> It seems to signal to the skies
> That blood of heroes never dies".

Moina Michael conceived an idea to wear red poppies on **Memorial Day,** in honor of those who died serving the nation during war. She was the first to wear one and sold poppies to her friends and co-workers with the money going to benefit servicemen and their families who were in need.

Madam Guerin from France visiting the United States learned of this new custom and when she returned to France she began making artificial red poppies to raise money for war orphans and widows. The tradition spread to other countries in 1921. Madam Guerin approached the VFW and they became the first veterans organization to sell poppies nationally.

Traditional observance of **Memorial Day** has diminished over the years. Many Americans have forgotten the meaning and traditions of Memorial Day. At many cemeteries the graves of the fallen are increasingly ignored and neglected. Most people no longer remember the proper flag etiquette for the day. Many people look to Memorial Day as a three day weekend holiday. There are still towns and cities that continue to hold Memorial Day parades and ceremonies. Our own Rhode Island Veterans Cemetery has a spectacular display of flags on Memorial Day. We should be proud of our heritage and keep it alive.

In 1951 the **Boy Scouts of America** began placing flags on the grave sites of the servicemen and women in our national cemeteries.

What we need to do is to return the **solemn and sacred spirit** back to **Memorial Day** and make it our traditional day of observance. The day that we honor our fallen heroes. In keeping with our **Memorial Day** celebration I would like to share with you the poem written by John McRae entitled **In Flanders Fields** That inspired the tradition of selling the poppy flower that I wear:

In Flanders Fields

In Flanders Fields the poppies grow.
Between the crosses, row by row,
That mark the place; and in the sky,
The larks still bravely, singing fly.
Scarce heard amid the guns below.

We are the dead short days ago.
We lived, fell down, saw sunset glow.

Loved and were loved, and now we lie
In Flanders Fields.

Take up our quarrel with the foe:
To you from falling hands we throw,
The torch: Be yours to hold on high,
If ye break faith with us who die,
We shall not sleep, though poppies grow,
In Flanders Fields. **John McCrae**

Traditionally we need to acknowledge and praise God for having allowed us the the freedom that we enjoy.

Scripture: *"May the Lord direct your hearts into God's love and Christ's perseverance." 2 Thessalonians 3:*

Closing prayer

FATHER'S DAY

Father's Day is Sunday, June 20th this year. Interestingly, June 20, 2010 marks the 100th anniversary of Father's Day. Have you ever wondered who started Father's Day and why is it so significant?

Although fathers have come a long way in a hundred years, some might say that they could again use an image boost . . . thanks to the antics of the likes of Brad Pitt, Tiger Woods and Jon Gosselin, to name a few. Perhaps it is easy to take pop-shots at men who mess up, but it is important to focus on the role that men play in our 21st century society and empower them and celebrate their achievements.

In 1908, in Spokane, Washington, a lady by the name of Sonora Dodd listened to the Pastor of her church, ramble on about the newly created Mother's Day and the importance of mothers. She told her pastor, "I liked everything you said about mothers and motherhood, but don't you think that fathers deserve a place in the sun, too?"

Sonora's father, William Smart, survived the Civil War and had moved West to seek his fortune. His wife died in the winter of 1898 while giving birth to their sixth child. But Mr. Smart with the help of Sonora, the eldest child, and the only girl, held the family together. She became convinced of the importance of her father and other fathers when at the time men were not considered very relevant to the family units.

It is obvious that William Smart made some unique sacrifices to keep his family together. It was tough and he worked very diligently at the task. But even in our own times, the 21st century, we are faced with some incredible challenges:

- In these days 15% of single parents are men.
- There were more than 158,000 stay-at-home Dads in 2009.
- 71% of 6 year olds had breakfast and dinner with their dads in 2006.
- Many fathers are good about reading to their children.
- Praising them regularly, taking them on outings, etc.

At the other extreme. statistics report:

- 90 Percent of homeless and runaway children are fatherless.
- 71 % of high school drop outs do not have a father.
- 63 percent of young people who commit suicide are from fatherless home.

A commentator recently wrote: "*Without concerned fathers, you would have no civilization.*"

Father's Day is hopefully a time when our culture says, "*This is our moment to look at our men and boys and recognize them for who they are.*" "*If we don't protect fathering we will serve to destroy our civilization.*"

Sonora Dodd certainly did her part to commemorate and promote Father's Day celebration. The first Father's Day was held in Spokane, Washington on June 20, 1910. Fathers in the church were honored by receiving a red rose, and people whose fathers were deceased wore white roses. Sonora Smart Dodd became the Mother of Father's Day.

Let's give praise to all of our fathers. God our Almighty Father and all of the fathers on this glorious day.

Prayer

WE THE PEOPLE, HAPPY FOURTH OF JULY

Our nation was founded 234 years ago in 1776 in Philadelphia, Pennsylvania. Since our Nation's founding, Americans have turned to prayer for inspiration, strength and guidance. In times of trial, we ask God for wisdom, courage, direction and comfort. We offer thanks for the countless blessings God has provided. We thank God for sanctifying every human life by creating each of us in His image. As we observe this National Holiday we call upon the Almighty to continue to bless America and her people.

George Washington prayed, *"Almighty God . . . We make our earnest prayer that Thou wilt keep the United States in Thy holy protection, and that Thou will incline the hearts of the citizens to cultivate a spirit of subordination and obedience to government, and entertain a brotherly affection and love for one another and for their fellow citizens of the United States. And finally, that Thou wilt most graciously be pleased to dispose us all to do justice, to love mercy, and to demean ourselves with that charity, humility, and pacific temper of mind which were the characteristics of the divine author of our blessed religion and without humble imitation of whose example is these thing we can never hope to be a happy nation. Grant our supplication, we beseach Thee, through Jesus Christ."* Since that day Americans have celebrated their independence on the **4th of July.**

The **Daily Atla California,** a newspaper wrote this about the 4th of July in **1855**
"Hallowed be the day, forever bright its memory,
In the heart of the Nation.
Sing to it poets,
Shout to it freedom,
Celebrate it with bonfires,
Parades and triumphant assemblies."
AND SO IT IS.

We gather together to watch and enjoy the fireworks displays. We have our local parades.

We join in picnics and cookouts. We come together to listen to patriotic speakers and candidates for political office. And we give thanks for our freedoms.

Comedian/actor **George Burns** said: "The secret to a good sermon is to have a good beginning, and a good ending . . . and have them as close together as possible."

> Scripture: *"If my people who are called by my name, will humble themselves and pray and seek my face, and turn from their wicked ways, then I will forgive their sins and will heal their land." 2nd Chronicles 7:14*

WHO IS PACKING YOUR PARACHUTE?

The story of **Charles Plumb, LT. USN Jet Pilot in Vietnam**

Charles Plumb, a Navy pilot, flew 75 combat missions over Vietnam. His plane was shot down by a surface-to-air missile during his last flight. Plumb ejected and parachuted into enemy territory.

He was captured and spent 6 years in a prison camp. He survived the ordeal and when he came home he toured the country lecturing on the lessons learned from his experiences.

One day when he and his wife were sitting in as restaurant having dinner, a man at a table near them got up and came over to their table. He introduced himself, and said, "Aren't you Lt. Plumb? You flew jet fighters in Vietnam off the aircraft carrier Kitty Hawk. I believe that you were shot down."

"How in the world did you know that?" asked Plumb.

"I packed your parachute," the man replied. Plumb gasped in surprise and gratitude.

The man pumped his hand and said, "I guess it worked."

Plumb assured him. "It certainly did work. If it hadn't opened we wouldn't be here today."

Plumb couldn't sleep that night wondering about that man. He said, "I kept wondering what did he look like in his Navy uniform: white hat, jumper with the big collar and bell bottom trousers." How could he have remembered me?

Plumb wondered how many times he had seen him and not even said, "**Good Morning**, or **How are you?**" "You see he was a Navy officer, Fighter Pilot and the man was just another sailor

Plumb thought of the man for many hours. How that sailor had worked so diligently in the parachute loft aboard the ship. Folding and carefully weaving the shrouds and folding the silk panels of the parachute, holding the fate of someone he didn't even know, each time he packed it.

The question is: "**Who is packing your chute?**"

Everyone has someone who provides that which we need to make it through the day.

We need many different kinds of parachutes. When Lt Plumb's jet was shot down he needed a **physical parachute** to get out of his disabled fighter. He also needed a **mental parachute,** and an **emotional parachute** as well as a **spiritual parachute.**

He relied on all of these supports before he reached safety. Even after he was captured and thrown into prison he continued to depend on those chutes.

Sometimes in the daily challenges that life gives us, we miss what really is important.

We may fail to say **hello . . . please . . . or thank you.** We may miss the opportunity to **congratulate someone,** or to acknowledge **something wonderful that has happened to them.** Or perhaps just giving someone a compliment or saying something nice, for no special reason, would help them through the day.

As you go through this week, this month this year, recognize and appreciate the people who pack your parachute. Next time you receive a friendly smile or a warm greeting consider that person is **"Packing your parachute."** Or better still, why don't you pack another person's **chute**? It truly works! 1 **Thessalonians 5:18** reads: "*No matter what happens, always be thankful, for it is God's will for you who belong to Christ Jesus*"

Closing prayer.

GIVE THANKS TO GOD—THANKSGIVING

Thanksgiving Day is a harvest festival. It is a time to give thanks for that which we have received through the bounty of God our Father. It is a holiday that is celebrated primarily in the United States and Canada. While it has a **religious** origin, Thanksgiving is now principally identified as a **secular holiday.**

It seems like the month of November is the bridge between two of the biggest commercial events of the year—**Halloween** and **Christmas**, with **Thanksgiving** stuck right in the middle. For many, Thanksgiving is a melody of **over eating;** turkey and dressing, cranberry sauce, mash-potatoes and gravy, including corn pudding, sweet potatoes, green beans, squash, followed by pumpkin pie or pecan pie with whipped cream. Hum, makes you hungry to think about it. Did you know that more than 300 million turkeys are raised in the United States each year with an estimated 40 million consumed on Thanksgiving Day?

In **1621**, after a hard and devastating first year in the New World, the Pilgrims' fall harvest was very successful and plentiful. There was corn, fruits, vegetables of all kinds, fish and meat that had been packed in salt or smoke cured over fires. They had enough food put away in stores to last through the coming winter.

The pilgrims had beaten the odds. They built homes in the wilderness, they raised enough crops to keep themselves alive, and they were at peace with their neighbors. **Governor William Bradford,** proclaimed a day of thanksgiving that was to be shared by all of the colonists and their neighboring native American Indians. And so it was.

The celebration of an annual gathering held following the harvest time went on for years. During the **American Revolution,** circa 1770, a day of national thanksgiving was suggested by the Continental Congress.

In **1863,** President Abraham Lincoln proclaimed a national day of thanksgiving, and since that time each President has issued a Thanksgiving proclamation, usually designating the fourth Thursday of November as the special holiday.

Thanksgiving is a time to thank God for all of the good things that he has bestowed upon us—the love and care of family members and friends; a healthy life; a successful career; caring children; and so many more blessings that we have received.

In celebration, I would like to share this story of a blessing entitled **"Secret Herb."**

It troubled Ben each time that he went to the kitchen and saw a little metal box sitting on the self above Martha's cook stove. He probably wouldn't have been so curious except Martha had repeatedly told him, **"Never touch the container."** The reason she said was that it contained a Secret Herb from her mother and she didn't want anyone to accidently drop it spilling the valuable contents.

The container wasn't much to look at. It was old and the colors had faded. But it had gotten a lot of use by Martha, her mother and her grand-mother. Martha never cooked without it. She would cook a dish and take the container from the shelf and sprinkle a little of the "secret herb" over the ingredients. Even when she baked cookies or cakes, or pies she would add a light sprinkle from the can before she put the dish in the oven.

Whatever was in the container sure worked because Ben felt that Martha was the best cook in the world. Anyone who came to eat at their house shared the same opinion. Somehow Martha had stretched the contents over 30 years of marriage. It never failed to work.

One day Martha fell ill, and Ben had to take her to the hospital where she was admitted. When Ben returned home he found the house extremely lonely. He went to the kitchen to see what was in the "fridge" and his eye caught the container on the shelf above the stove.

Curiosity nagged him. What was in the container? Why wasn't he allowed to touch it? Finally, he couldn't resist the urge to look in it. He carefully took it off the shelf, and opened the lid. The container was empty except for a folded slip of paper on the bottom. He slowly unfolded it and read the note. Scrawled inside in Martha's handwriting it simply said, **"Martha—To Everything You Make, Add a Dash of Love."**

Now Ben understood why Martha's cooking tasted so good.

As so it is with our celebrating **Thanksgiving.** We need to take a little of Martha's seasoning and add it to our Thanksgiving dish. And you will certainly be blessed

Prayer.

RHUBARB

The origin of the plant named **Rhubarb** is from the Greek, **Rha,** which is the ancient name of the Volga River, along whose banks the plants grew, plus the word **barbarous.** It is described as a plant having long green and red stalks that are edible when sweetened with sugar and cooked.

It also is called the pie plant. Where the body of the word, barbarous, came from is unknown but it may be because although the stalks are good, the leaves contain **oxalic acid** and can therefore be very toxic. They are poisonous.

Rhubarb is generally eaten as a fruit, but botanically it is a vegetable. Because of its intense tartness rhubarb is usually combined with considerable amounts of sugar. It makes delicious sauces, jams, and pies. (Thus the name **pie plant.**) In America a traditional flavor combination is rhubarb and strawberries. In England, rhubarb and ginger. It has a fair amount of Vitamin A.

Another definition of **rhubarb,** in an informal sense is: **A quarrel, a fight, or a heated discussion.** We do know that this usage was popularized by baseball. The Oxford English Dictionary has the first citation in 1943. Mr. "Red" Barber, sports announcer for the Brooklyn Dodgers baseball team used the term rhubarb to describe an argument or a mix up on the field of play. The word may also have a connection with **"hey rube"** used to describe a circus brawl or an incident in the theatre.

In any event, I love rhubarb pie. Make it strawberry-rhubarb and that is even better. Or I may even settle for some rhubarb sauce. I don't know if it is the tartness or the sweet taste but it is good. Boy it is good!

When we moved from Illinois to Connecticut, my Father-in-Law insisted that we take a bushel basket of rhubarb roots to plant at our new home. I carefully planted them in the garden but had no success. I tried for several years and finally, on my last try, the plants took root and we had a beautiful rhubarb harvest with healthy stalks growing next to our asparagus and tomato plants.

My wife who's father-in-law was a dairy farmer, tells the story of what his experience was with rhubarb. He claimed that he could plant of field of alfalfa and turn his herd loose in the field and if there was one patch of rhubarb standing in the field the cows would eat all of the alfalfa but never eat the luscious green leaves of the rhubarb. They knew better.

What I have learned about rhubarb has provided me with several little object lessons:

1. **Even dumb animals know that it is unwise to eat the foliage of rhubarb.** We know the Lord is there to watch after us and keep us safe if only we allow him to do so.
    "The angel of the Lord encamps around those who fear him, he delivers them."
    Palm 34:7

2. **Rhubarb needs to go through a cold season in order to flourish.** As Christians we need to go through cold times, times of trial in order to develop spiritually.
    "Consider it pure joy, my brothers, whenever you face trials of many kinds, because you know that testing of your faith develops perseverance."
    James 1:3

3. **The leaves are poisonous and need to be cut away from the stalk.** As followers of Jesus, certain things have to be cut away from our lives as we walk with Him. *"Everyone who confesses the name of the Lord must turn away from wickedness."*
    2 Timothy 2:19

4. **For the best rhubarb desserts, you must add sugar or honey.** When we accept Christ, the Holy Spirit enters our hearts and because of his presence in our lives we are changed as we bear fruit of the Spirit.
    *"The fruit of the Spirit is **love, peace, patience, kindness, goodness, faithfulness, gentleness and self control.** Against such things there is no law."*
    Galatians 5:22-25

Prayer: Dear loving creator, sustain me, cleanse me, change me. Amen

WHEAT AND WEEDS TOGETHER

When the month of August finally arrives we see a dramatic change in the vegetable gardens and flower gardens around our house. Depending on the daily temperatures, the amount of rain and how diligent we have been in keeping the gardens weeded, we will have a beautiful and enjoyable sight or a rather foreboding, depressing mess.

Jesus challenges us when we read Matthew 13: 16-17 *"Blessed are your eyes because they see, and your ears because they hear." "For I tell you the truth, many prophets and righteous men longed to see what you see, but did not see it, and to hear what you hear but did not hear it."*

Then Jesus tells the parable of the sower. Remember the definition of a parable ?

"An Earthly Story with a Heavenly meaning." Jesus used parables as an effective way to teach and to make an everlasting point Listen then to what the parable of the sower means:

> A farmer went out to sow his seed. As he was scattering the seed some fell along the pathway.
>
> And the birds came and ate it up. Some fell on rocky places, where it did not have much soil.

It sprang up quickly because the soil was shallow. But when the sun came up the plants were scorched and they withered because they had no roots. Other seed fell among the thorns which grew up and choked the plants. Still other seeds fell on good soil where it produced a bumper crop

So what does that mean to us? How can we relate to this? Jesus continues in vs 19-23 to explain the morale of the story::

> *"When anyone hears the message about the kingdom and does not understand it, the evil one comes and snatches away*

what was sown in his heart. This is the seed sown along the path. The one who received the seed that fell on rocky places is the man who hears the word and at once receives it with joy. But because he has no root, he lasts only a short time. When trouble or persecution comes because of the word he quickly falls away. The one who received the seed that fell among the thorns is the man who hears the word, but worries of this life and the deceitfulness of wealth, chokes it and make it unfruitful. But the one who received the seed that fell on good soil is the man who hears the word and understands it. He produces a crop yielding a hundred sixty or thirty times what was sown. Matthew 13:19-23.

As we more fully understand the objective of the lesson we look out and see the gardens that we planted in the spring and wonder what we are to do. What about all those weeds?

Ralph Waldo Emerson defines a weed as, **"A plant whose virtues have not been discovered."**

Jesus told another parable. The parable of the weeds. He said:

"The Kingdom of heaven is like a man who sowed good seed in his field. But while everyone was sleeping, his enemy came and sowed weeds among the wheat, and went away. When the wheat sprouted and formed heads, then the weeds also appeared.

The owner's servants came to him and said, "Sir didn't you sow good seed in your field? Where did the weeds come from?

An enemy did this, he replied. The servants asked him, "Do you want us to go and pull them up?" No, he answered, because while you are pulling the weeds you may root up the wheat with them. Let both grow together until harvest. At that time I tell the harvesters : First collect the weeds and tie them in bundles to be burned. Then gather the wheat and bring it into my barn

Jesus explained this parable of the Weeds in the Field as:

The one who sowed the good seed is the Son of Man. The field is the World and
The good seed stands for the sons of the kingdom. The weeds are the sons of the
Evil one and the enemy who sows them is the devil. The harvest is the end of the
Age and the harvesters are angels.

As the weeds are pulled up and burned in the fire, so it will be at the end of the age.
The Son of Man will send out his angels and they will weed out of his kingdom. everything that causes sin and all who do evil. They will throw them into the fiery furnace, where there will be weeping and gnashing of teeth.

Then the righteous will shine like the sun in the kingdom of their Father.
He who has ears, let him hear. Matthew 13: 37-43

Closing Prayer

TWINKIES AND ROOT BEER

A little boy wanted to meet God. He knew it was a long trip to where God lived, so he packed his suitcase with **Twinkies** and a six pack of **Root Beer**—and he started on his journey.

When he had gone three blocks he met an elderly man. The man was sitting in the park just feeding the pigeons. The boy sat down next to him and opened his suitcase. He was about to take a drink from his Root Beer when he noticed the man looked hungry, so he offered him a Twinkie. The man gracefully accepted it and smiled at the boy. His smile was so pleasant that the boy wanted to see it again so he offered him a Root Beer.

Again the man smiled at him. The boy was delighted. They sat there all afternoon eating and smiling, but never said a word.

As it grew dark, the boy realized how tired he was and he got up to leave. Before he had gone more than a few steps he turned around and ran back to the man and gave him a big hug. The man gave him his biggest smile.

When the boy arrived home, his mother was surprised by the look of joy on his face. She asked "What did you do today that made you so happy?"

"I had lunch with God," he said. But before his mother could respond he added, "You know what, God's got the most beautiful smile I have ever seen."

Meanwhile, the elderly man, also radiant with joy, returned to his home. His son was stunned by the look of peace on his face and asked, "Dad, what did you do today that made you so happy?" He replied, "I ate Twinkies in the park with God. And you know he is much younger than I had expected."

Too often we underestimate the power of a touch, a smile, a kind word, a listening ear, an honest compliment or the smallest act of caring. All of which have the potential to turn a life around. People come into our lives for a reason, a season or a lifetime. It is important to let people know that they have a special way. Let them know how important it is to **Have Lunch with God.**

Prayer

> **Scripture:** Jesus teaching about humility in Luke 14: 11 says: **"For the proud will be humbled—but the humble will be honored."**

Do Not Worry About Life

Luke tells of what Jesus said in, Luke 12: 22-24.

"Therefore I tell you, do not worry about your life, what you will eat or about your body, what you will wear. Life is more than food and the body more than clothes. Consider the ravens; They do not sow or reap, they have no store room or barn; yet God feeds them. And how much more valuable you are than the birds! Who of you by worrying can add a single hour to your life? Since you cannot do this very little thing, why do you worry."

A young lady was worrying and complaining to her father about how difficult her life had become. No matter what she did, she said, it never seemed to work out right.

The father didn't say anything. He simply took her to the kitchen and set three pans of water on the stove. As each pan began to boil he added something to it. The first pan he added carrots.

To the second pan he added eggs and to the third pan he added ground coffee.

After all three pans had cooked a while he put their contents into separate bowls and asked his daughter to cut into eggs and the carrots and smell the coffee. "Okay" said his daughter, "What does this all mean?" She asked rather impatiently.

"Each food." he said, "Teaches us something about adversity and why we need not worry."

The carrot went into the boiling water hard but came out soft and weak. The eggs went in fragile but came out hardened. The coffee, however. changed the water to something better."

Which will <u>you</u> be like as you face life? Will you give up and become soft, or will you become tough and hard—or will you not worry and let God simply transform adversity into triumph? As the chef of your own life what will you bring to the table?"

Prayer

SLEEP WHEN THE RAINS COME

The month of April has been one of the wettest months for more than 100 years in the State of Rhode Island. Meteorologists and historians have agreed that the deluge of rain received in the last few days of March and the beginning of April was unprecedented. The flood waters came up so fast that many families didn't have time to get out of their homes. One resident was heard to say, "I'm not leaving without my dog." Another home owner said. "It sounds like Niagara Falls in my basement."

Roads were turned into rivers, low level land became lakes, bridges were washed out and roads became impassable. Merchants in West Warwick found themselves submerged in water, inventories lost, and their businesses closed.

Basements that had always been dry ended up with 24 to 48 inches of water. Some residents are still using sump pumps while pulling wet trash out of their cellars. If it happens again in another 100 years it will be too soon. With the events of this spring still fresh in our memories we may have a better appreciation of Noah and his Ark and the forty-days of rain that flooded the world. What we do know is God promised that He would never destroy the world with another flood. Some think that he was coming close again this time.

Now that the sun is shining again and the waters are receding I am reminded of the story of the farmer and his hired hand who slept when the rains came.

A farmer owned land along a fertile valley and he needed a hired hand to help him with his work. He advertised for help but most people were reluctant to work on the farm because of the risk of being flooded out when the spring rainy season came. They dreaded the storms and the havoc on the buildings and crops.

As the farmer interviewed applicants for the job, he received a steady stream of refusals.

Finally, a short thin man, well past middle age, approached the farmer. "Are you a good farm hand?" asked the farmer. *"Well I sleep when the rains come,"* answered the little man.

Although puzzled by the answer, the farmer, desperate for help, hired him. The littler man worked well around the farm, busy from dawn to dusk. The farmer felt satisfied with the man's work. He was pleased that he had hired this person.

Then one night the wind began to howl. Black rain clouds filled the sky. Lightning flashed is all quadrants. It began to rain and the rain turned to torrents. The farmer jumped out of bed, grabbed a light and rushed next door to the hired hand's sleeping quarters. He shook the little man and yelled, **"Get up! A storm is coming! We need to get things to higher ground!"**

The little man rolled over in bed and said firmly, *"No sir. I told you that I sleep when the rains come."*

Enraged by the response the farmer was tempted to fire him on the spot. Instead, he hurried outside to prepare for the storm. He discovered that all of the farm equipment had been moved to higher ground. Sand bags had been filled and placed around the barn. The cows and chickens had been moved to a shelter above the flood plain. Everything possible had been done in preparation of the flood.

The farmer then understood what his hired hand meant, so he returned to bed to sleep while the rains came.

When you are prepared spiritually, mentally and physically you have nothing to worry or fear.

The hired hand had secured the farm against the storm as best he could. We can secure ourselves against the storms of life by grounding ourselves in the **Word of God.**

We don't need to understand, we just need to hold His hand in order to have peace in the middle of the storm.

> The Bible says: *I lift my eyes to the hills—from where will my help come?*
> *My help comes from the Lord, who made heaven and earth.*
> *He will not let your foot be moved, He who keeps you will not slumber.*

The Lord will keep you from all evil, He will keep your life. The Lord will keep you going out and coming in from this time on and forever. Psa. 121: 1-3, 7-8.

Closing prayer.

IMPATIENCE AND RUDENESS VS. LOVE

Scripture: 1 Cor. 13: 5, 7 *"Love is . . . not rude, it is not self-seeking, it is not angered. It keeps no records of wrong doing. It always protects, always trusts, always hopes, always perseveres."*

The light turned yellow just as the driver approached the intersection. He did the right thing, stopping at the crosswalk, even though he could have beaten the red light by accelerating through the intersection.

The tailgating woman driver behind him slammed on her brakes, laid on the horn and began screaming in frustration. She had missed her chance to get through the light without having to stop and in the process she had dropped her cell phone, her coffee and her makeup on the floor of the car. Not to mention the two bags of groceries that had been sitting on the back seat.

She was still in a tantrum when she heard a tap on the window and looked up into the face of a very serious police officer. The officer polity ordered her to **"Get out of the car with your hands up."** He took her to the police station where she was searched, fingerprinted, photographed and placed in a holding cell.

After a couple of hours the jailer approached the cell and opened the door. She was escorted back to the booking desk where the arresting officer was waiting with her personal effects.

He said, "I'm very sorry for the mistake ma'm. You see I pulled up behind your car while you were **blowing your horn, flipping off the guy in front of you, and cursing a blue streak.** I noticed the *What Would Jesus Do?* bumper sticker, the *Choose Life* license plate holder, the *Follow Me To Sunday School* bumper slogan, and the chrome-plated *Christian Fish* emblem on the trunk.

So naturally . . . . I assumed you had stolen the car."

Lesson: No matter what we do or what we say we are always God's representative and we need to act accordingly.

Prayer of Saint Francis of Assisi

Lord make me an instrument of your peace. Where there is hatred, let me sow love.

Where there is injury, pardon. Where there is doubt, faith. Where there is despair, hope.

Where there is darkness, light. And where there is sadness, joy.

How many times in a single day do we have an opportunity to witness? Maybe it is a simple smile or a friendly greeting, or to help someone with a grocery cart or a heavy package. Often it is our basic personal demeanor that makes the difference. Ask yourself this question:

WHAT WOULD JESUS DO? And then do it.

Prayer

No Ordinary Day

When my children were young and still at home, we lived in a house located in Bloomfield, Connecticut.

We had about three acres of land and a small brook meandered through the back section. It wasn't deep enough to swim in and there weren't any fish to catch but the brook was home to hundreds of tadpoles who by the 4th of July each year were considered fair game for our annual 4th of July Family Picnic and Frog Jumping Contest.

It was a tradition for the boys, and their father, to go out in the morning of the 4th, before the guests arrived, and with a couple of nets we would catch twenty or thirty frogs and put them in several large plastic buckets. We were careful not to harm the frogs. There is nothing more frustrating than to get a handicapped frog for the big frog jumping contest.

About noon the guests would start to arrive, the picnic began with all of the food and embellishments, and we all enjoyed a "Red White and Blue Celebration" including blueberry pie, cherry pie and vanilla ice cream.

Then it came time for the big event. No fireworks, sparklers or fire crackers. It was time for the Frog Jumping Contest. All of the children would line up on a line, parallel to the brook, at a distance of about forty feet, and wait to get their frog. Each person had a large paper cup and the officials would carry the bucket of frogs down the line and put a frog under each cup. With a Ready, Set, Go, the contest began. At the command Go, the paper cup was lifted and the race was on.

The rules were simple: No one could touch the frog, kick it, or pick it up and throw it. You could get down on your knees and yell at the frog. You could slap the ground behind it to make it jump towards the brook. You might even try blowing on its rump. Anything to make it move. The object was to have your frog get back into the water first. One year we had enough kids that we ran several heats, with the final winners receiving a first, second and third prize.

But, you can't imagine the things that happened. One little girl lifted her cup, released the frog and the critter jumped right back into her lap. You can imagine the reaction and horror that resulted. One of the kids had a frog who wouldn't move. It must have been traumatized by all of the confusion. One of the boys was trying to get his frog to jump by pounding on the ground behind it. It wouldn't go quickly enough so the boy began to stomp on the ground behind it, Oops, a misjudged stomp smashed the frog into the turf. That required a replacement frog.

One year we had an exceptionally dry spring. The brook was also dry. No frogs in sight. What could we do? Not far from the house was a small pond so we went to the pond to catch frogs.

We were successful, we got a dozen or so. Some were even larger and more active than the ones we had in our brook. That was a fun day because we had to run several heats, catching the frogs that made it to the brook and running them again in the next race, three or four times. By the end of the day we had some pretty worn out frogs. It was no ordinary day for the frogs, and certainly no ordinary day for the kids, and the adults as well. And so it was.

> *"How great is the love the Father has lavished on us, that we*
> *should be called children of God! And that is what we are."*
> *1 John 3:1a (NIV)*

There are no **Ordinary Days** for a child of God. We are daily lavished with God's extraordinary love and grace. Trusting, childlike eyes see wonders showered on us even in the most unexpected places.

The Apostle Paul wrote a letter to the Church at Corinth. A new church that he had started some two to three years prior. He was concerned for them because he heard reports of strife and division threatening the young church. Some had become spirituality arrogant leading to misconduct against other believers. Paul wrote seeking to restore balance to the church.

In chapter 13: 4-7, Paul reminds us of our relationship with God and explains the love we have and how it works

> *"Love is patient, love is kind.*
> *It does not envy, it does not boast.*
> *It is not proud. It is not rude.*

It is not seeking. It is not easily angered.
It keeps no record of wrongs.
Love does not delight in evil but rejoices with the truth.
It always protects, always trusts.
Always hopes, and always perseveres."

I trust that this hasn't been an **Ordinary Day** for you. I pray that you will languish in God's **Love** and **Grace.**

Prayer

Be Good And Joyful Always

Sometimes we find ourselves in an very precarious position. A situation develops and we don't know just what to say or do. Perhaps this story may help teach us what to do if we are truly believers.

The Story:

A mother took her two children to a restaurant for dinner. Her six year old son asked if he could say grace. The mother acknowledged and they bowed their heads in prayer.

The little boy started: "God is great, God is good . . . we thank you for the food. I would thank you even more if Mom would get us some ice cream for dessert. And liberty and justice for all." Amen.

Along with laughter from the other customers nearby, a woman remarked: "That is what is wrong with this country. Kids today don't even know how to pray.(Humph) Asking God for ice cream, well, I never."

Hearing the laughter and the remark made by the woman the little boy burst into tears. "What did I do wrong? Is God mad at me?" He said.

His mother held him and assured him that he had done no wrong, and that he had done a terrific job. "Certainly God was not mad at you," she said. Just then an elderly man approached the table. He winked at the mother and smiled at the boy and said, "I happen to know that God thinks that was a great prayer."

"Really?" the boy said. "Do you really think so?"

"Cross my heart," the man replied.

Then, in a low whisper, he added, (referring to the woman whose remark started the whole thing,) "Too bad she never asks God for ice cream. A little ice cream is sometimes good for the soul."

Naturally, the mother bought ice cream for the kids at the end of the meal. But the six-year-old boy stared at his dish of ice cream for a moment, and then did something that his mother and those at the nearby tables will never forget.

He picked up the sundae and without saying a word, walked over to the woman's table and placed it in front of her. Then with a big smile he told her, "Here, this is for you. Ice Cream is good for the soul sometimes, and my soul is good already."

In the New Testament book of ***Titus*** the apostle Paul writes to his young friend Titus a short letter giving him guidelines for a godly life—including relationships between family, friends and society, with an emphasis on faith that overcomes division and disharmony.

Titus 3:1-2 provides us the answer that was demonstrated by the little boy in our story.

> Paul says,
> ***"Remind the people to be subject to rulers and authorities, to be obedient, to be ready to do whatever is good, to slander no one, to be peaceable and considerate and to show true humility toward all men."***

Amen.

Closing prayer

DADDY'S EMPTY CHAIR

Scripture: 1 John 5:14-15 **This is the boldness we have in him, that if we ask anything according to his will, he hears us. And if we know that he hears us in whatever we ask we know that we have obtained the requests made of him.**

A man's daughter ask the local minister to come and pray with her father. When the pastor arrived he found the man lying in bed with his head propped up on two pillows. An empty chair sat beside the bed. The minister assumed that the old fellow had been informed of his visit. "I guess you were expecting me," he said.

No! who are you? asked the man. The minister told him his name and who he was and remarked, "I saw the empty chair and I figured you knew I was going to visit with you." the minister said.

"Oh yeah, the chair" the bedridden man said. "Would you mind closing the door?" Puzzled, the minister shut the door. "I have never told anyone this," said the man, "Not even my daughter."

"But all of my life I have never known how to pray. At church I used to listen to the preacher talk about prayer, but it went right over my head. I abandoned any attempt at prayer."

But, one day about fours ago my best friend Jimmy said to me . . . "Prayer is just a simple matter of having a conversation with God. Here is what I suggest, **Sit down in a chair, place an empty chair in front of you and in faith, see Jesus on the chair.**

It is not spooky, because he promised, *"I will be with you always."* Then just speak to him in the same way you're doing with me right now.

"So, I tried it and I've liked it so much that I do it a couple of hours every day. I'm careful though. If my daughter saw me talking to an empty chair, she's either have a heart-attack or send me off to the "funny farm."

The minister was deeply moved by the story and encouraged the old man to continue on his journey. Then he took the man's hand and prayed with him and returned to the church.

Two nights later the daughter called to inform the minister that her daddy had died that afternoon.

"Did he die in peace?" asked the minister. **Yes!**, when I left the house about two o'clock he called me over to the bedside, told me he loved me and kissed me on the cheek. When I got back from the store an hour later I found him . . . .

There was something strange about his death. Apparently, just before Daddy died he leaned over and rested his head on the chair beside the bed. What do you make of that?

The minister smiled gently and wiped a tear from his eye and said, "I wish we could all go like that."

Prayer is one of the best **free gifts** we receive.

I asked God for water, He gave me an ocean.
I asked God for a flower, He gave me a garden.
I asked God for a friend, He gave me all of you.
If God brings you to it, he will bring you through it.

Happy moments, praise God.
Difficult moments, seek God.
Quiet moments, worship God
Painful moments, trust God.
Every moment thank God.

Prayer

THE HALLOWS OF HALLOWEEN

Halloween dates back many thousands of years to the ancient Celtics **(Kelts)** who lived in what is now Great Britain, Ireland, and northern France. The celebration was the biggest and most significant holiday of the Celtic year. It was the beginning of their new year which came on November first.

Celtic legends tell us that on the eve of the new year, all the hearth fires in Ireland would be extinguished, and then re-lit from the central fire of the **Druids at Tlachtga,** 12 miles from the royal hill of **TARA,** which was the centre of Celtic religious worship.

The Druids were the leaders and the learned-class among the Celts. They were the religious priests who acted as judges, lawmakers, poets, scholars, and scientists. Upon sacred bonfires the Druids burned animals and crops as tributes to their pagan Gods. The extinguishing of the hearth fires symbolized the **"dark half"** of the year. Then the re-kindling of the cooking fires from the Druid fire was symbolic of the returning life that was hoped for in the coming Spring. The feast was known as the feast of Samhain **(sow-en).**

In the Celtic belief system was the **"turning point,"** such things as the time between one day and the next, the meeting of the sea and the shore, the turning of one year into the next, were all seen as magical times. They also believed that the fires would ward off the increased darkness that came with winter and thereby keep them alive and safe. And so it has became a tradition that we recognize, even today.

On October 31, we will likely see witches, ghosts, goblins, skeletons, demons and other evil characters knocking at our door, hollering "Trick or Treat." And they will expect a treat or we will be tricked. So as a tradition we will have ready apples, and candies and all kinds of goodies. There will be decorated jack-o-lanterns, witches on brooms, big black cats and nasty looking rats. It is the one day of the year when we give free food to strangers to keep them from vandalizing our property. And we ask . . . **"Where did we get this celebration called Halloween?"**

When the Romans conquered England and Ireland, their custom of commemorating the passing of the dead in late October became intertwined with the Celtic holiday. The Roman holiday was called **Pomona Day.** Centuries later Christianity spread into Celtic lands and in **800 AD** Pope Boniface IV wanted to eliminate the pagan aspects of the holiday and he re-named the festival "**All Saints or All Souls Day.**" This was later changed to "**Hallow Mass or All Hallows.**" Later, the name became **Halloween.** It was celebrated with big bonfires, parades, people dressed in costumes like angels or devils and included the carving of gourds, potatoes and squash. But no pumpkins.

The pumpkin is a New World plant that never grew in Europe until modern times, so it couldn't have been used to make Jack O Lanterns by the Druids. Pumpkins are fruits. A pumpkin is a type of squash and is a member of the gourd family, (**Cucurbitacae**) (cu-curbit-a-cay) which also includes cucumbers, gherkins and melons.

Although the English had previously carved faces into turnips or potatoes to ward off the evils spirits it was Americans who first carved pumpkins which are native to North America.

Pumpkins are low in calories, fat and sodium and high in fiber. They are a good source of Vitamin A, B, Potassium and Iron. They can be found everywhere in the country from doorsteps to dinner tables. Despite the widespread carving that goes on every autumn, few people know the story of how the pumpkin compares to being a Christian.

A Sunday School teacher explained to her students: "A Christian is like being a pumpkin. God picks you from the patch . . . . brings you in . . . . washes off all the dirt. Then he cuts the top off and scoops out all the yucky stuff. He removes the seeds of fear, doubt, despair, hate, impurity and greed. Then He carves you a new smiling face and puts His light inside of you to shine for all the world to see."

Today the devils and ghosts and goblins are still an important part of **Halloween,** but the holiday has lost much of its religious connotation. Now on **Halloween Eve** kids stretch their legs, fly on brooms and fight evil forces.

Nighttime trickery gets sweeter with every stop as miniature Snicker bars, and Tootsie Rolls fill up plastic sacks, pillowcases and shopping bags.

So, let's enjoy the holiday. Have a happy **Halloween.** While we celebrate keep in mind this scripture from Titus:

"The grace of God that brings salvation has appeared to all men. It teaches us to say "No" to ungodliness and worldly passions, and to live self-controlled, upright and godly lives in this present age."
Titus 2:11-12

Closing prayer: Lord thank you for another day within this life of mine. Give me the strength to live it well.

Whatever I may find, help me to be strong and courageous, not be discouraged, for I know you are with me where ever I go. Amen.

DELIGHTS OF AUTUMN

I am a Jack O Lantern
My light will shine so bright.
For I am a Christian pumpkin
My symbols tell what's right.

My nose is like the cross
On which the Savior died,
To set us free from sin
We need no longer hide.

My mouth is like a fish
The whole wide world to show,
That Christians live in this house
And love their Savior so!

The story starts at Christmas
My eyes are like the star,
That shone on Baby Jesus
And wise men saw from afar.

My color it orange
Just like the big bright sun,
That rose on Easter Day
Along with God's own Son.

And so on Halloween
Let's set our pumpkin out,
And tell the trick-or-treaters . . .
What God's love is all about

Author unknown

To All Who Flew Behind Round Engines

R1820, R1830, R985, R2800, R3350, and especially R4360s

We must get rid of those turbine engines. They are ruining aviation, not to mention our hearing and our dignity. A turbine engine is too simple-minded and has little or no mystery. Intake air starts at the front, travels through it in a straight line and doesn't pick up any of the pungent fragrance of engine oil or pilot sweat like a round engine.

Anyone can start a turbine engine. You just move the switch from "OFF" to "START" and then remember to move it back to "ON" after a while. My personal computer is harder to start than a turbine.

Cranking a round engine requires skill, finesse, and style. You have to seduce it into starting. A lot depends on the temperature and humidity and the direction of the wind. On some types of airplanes the pilots aren't even allowed to start them.

Turbine engines start by whining for a little while, then give a lady like poof and start whining a little louder. Round engines, after being primed and pampered, start with a rattle-rattle, click-click BANG, a puff of gray smoke, more rattles another BANG, a macho FART or two, more clicks, a lot more smoke and it finally settles down in a serious low pitched roar. We like that. It's a guy thing.

When you start a round engine, your mind is engaged and you can concentrate on the flight ahead. Starting a turbine is like flicking on a ceiling fan. Nice but hardly exciting. It just doesn't get your adrenalin pumping.

It doesn't take a new pilot long to learn it is not a good idea to walk behind an airplane starting with round engines. That new white uniform shirt will be covered with black oil specks from thirty yards.

When you have started those round engines successfully, your crew chief or flight engineer will look up at you like he'd also let you kiss his girl friend,

Turbines don't break or catch on fire often enough, which leads the aircrew to boredom, complacency and inattention. A round engine, at cruise, looks and sounds like it's going to blow up at any minute. This keeps the pilot's attention focused on the operation

Turbine engines don't have enough control levers, mixer, prop, feather levers, and an assortment of round gauges for the pilots to tap on and give them something to do. There is nothing to fiddle with, you can't adjust the mixer, synch the propellers, reset the manifold pressure and monitor the cylinder head, and oil pressure gauges. Boring!

And, don't forget the outside air temperature and visible moisture that can develop carburetor or injection icing. Better keep an eye on that.

Round engines sling a wicked hunk of metal known as a propeller. Ask anyone from Hamilton-Standard about the nostalgia of those chromed blades and polished spinners. You really haven't experienced it until you have heard the ice coming off those blades and hitting the fuselage. It's like the sound of Woody Wood Pecker working on a dead tree on a summer evening.

Round engines love oil. It just isn't right unless it takes two gallons of oil per engine after a three hour trip. Turbine engines don't use oil. But, they smell like a Boy Scout camp full of Coleman lanterns. Round engines smell like God intended machines to smell. Robust.

Round engines generally fly low enough so that the crew can keep one eye on the ground and the other eye on the base of the growing thunderstorms ahead.

But, don't operate a turbine below 10,000 feet with out double checking the fuel state and weight and balance. That is why turbine drivers use "pounds of fuel" instead of gallons

Ever hear a round engine driver talk about "Burn Out"? No, he isn't thinking of quitting He is leaning out the engine with the mixture control to make the engine, running at idle RPM, burn the carbon deposits off the spark plugs. Unheard of in a turbine engine operation.

We have only brushed the surface of Round vs. Turbine. But, the bottom line is turbine engines have to go, round engines need to be remembered. What will we talk to our grandkids about if it isn't the sanctity of the round engine? Consider this as a tribute to your experience as a round engine operator. Happy landings.

Al Schmid
ATP 1345745
(Just 1.3 Million Short of the Wright Brothers)

IT'S TOUGH TO BRING A HELLCAT DOWN

After reading a story entitled **Fast, Cheap and Out of Control,** by Peter Merlin, I was reminded of a similar flight of a Grumman F6F Hellcat from Chincoteague, Va. in 1956.

Utility Squadron Four, VU-4, operated from NAS Chincoteague, Va. (Now known as Wallops Island, NASA.) VU-4's mission was to provide flights for Navy ships operating off the mid-Atlantic coast, conducting CIC (Combat Information Center) Radar training, and Radar Controlled Anti-Aircraft Fire support. First came the radar vectoring, followed by a sleeve towed by an airplane, and finally a real live shoot-out using a full sized WWII fighter made by Grumman Aircraft.

More than 12,000 F6F Hellcats were built between 1942 and 1945. It was one of the most successful fighters flown by the Navy. It was simple, rugged and could take a great deal of punishment. Making the Hellcat into a drone airplane in the early 50's was a good idea. Just paint the airplane red, install a remote controlled auto pilot and it became a perfect flying target. After ten hours of proving flights with a safety pilot on board the drone was ready to serve the mission as a NOLO, No Live Pilot On Board target.

Flying a chase airplane, known as "Charlie" on a drone shoot was exciting and almost like being engaged in actual combat. The squadron was very experienced in drone shoots, operating one airplane that had survived 25 missions, returning home with gaping holes and flak damage, but still flying.

On one particular day the drone shoot became a memorable event. The F6F was preflighted, ground checked and put into the launch position. Charlie 1, 2 and 3 came swooping down to pickup the airplane as "Fox", the ground controller, added power for the take off. All went well and it was a picture-book launch. The Hellcat climbed like a home sick angel. The group was on its way to rendezvous with a ship located in Warning Area 387A about 150 miles east of Cape Charles. VA.

Climb out appeared to be routine until Charlie 1 reported that he could not get the airplane to respond to his inputs. Charlie 2 and then Charlie 3 tried without success. The airplane was climbing with climb power and it continued until it reached its service ceiling, about 13,500 feet. As it leveled off it began a lazy turn to the left. It was almost as though the airplane was saying, "I'm happy right here boys, I'm not going anywhere with you."

Lt. Steinbring, Charlie 1, called base operations on his radio and reported the difficulty. The Operations Duty Officer went through a check list of items to try to correct the problem. No luck. Finally, the OPS Officer ordered the group to shoot the drone down.

The F8F Bearcats flown by the chase pilots were armed with twin 50 caliber machine guns. The Hellcat was a sitting duck. What a break to shoot down one of your own airplanes.

Charlie I, then Charlie 2 and finally Charlie 3 made numerous runs on the drone. They could not shoot it down. In fact, they used up all of their ammunition. In desperation they reported the situation to Operations. After a conference with Captain White, the commanding officer of VU-4, a decision was made to call the Air Force to see if they could destroy the drone.

Can you imagine what went through the mind of the Operations Officer at Langley Air Force Base at Newport News, Va. when he received this call? Unbelievable! The Air Force is going to shoot down a US Navy fighter. A dream come true. Unfortunately, the Duty Officer did not have the authority to launch any fighter to intercept the drone. He had to get orders from Washington. He was on the phone in a flash.

Meanwhile, the drone continued to make circles at 13,000 feet and the prevailing westerly winds were blowing it further and further out to sea. Lt. Steinbring decided to try his auto pilot control again, and eureka, the drone responded. By now the group had used up a lot of fuel and it was determined that it would be unwise to try and get it back home.

The decision was to ditch the airplane in the sea. Lt. Cunningham, Charlie two had always wondered what it would be like to make an emergency landing at sea. He took control and remotely flew the airplane down to the surface, extended the wing flaps and with the landing gear still up landed the airplane in a swell.

The landing was perfect. After the splash the airplane seemed to bob to the surface and began to float. Lt. Cunningham reported later that **if** he had been on board he would have had time to get out of his harness, inflate the raft, and climb into it without even getting his feet wet.

Now the airplane became a hazard to surface vessels. What can be done? After about twelve minutes the F6F slowly sank below the surface. A final tribute to a tough, rugged fighter that didn't give up easily.

It is tough to bring a Hellcat down.

Al Schmid
USNR 575719

Fly On Wings of An Eagle

The mother eagle teaches her chicks to fly by making their nest so uncomfortable that they are forced to leave it and commit themselves to the unknown world outside. The eagle's nest is sometimes nine feet in diameter and weighs as much as two tons. With from one to three eaglets in the nest, one would think there would be plenty of room.

But, for the eagle to survive it must learn to fly. At about eight weeks of age the father and mother eagles stop bringing food to the nest. Instead, they fly up to the nest and leave scrapes. The eaglets call for food eagerly but the parents make it so uncomfortable that eventually the young eagle stands on the edge of the nest and flaps its wings. The parents fly by with tidbits of food and coax it into the air. Lifted by a light wind it becomes airborne, flying—or gliding—for the first time in its life. It sails across the valley to make a scrambling, almost tumbling landing on a bare knoll.

And so it is with God. God does that to us. He stirs up our comfortable nests, pushes or coaxes us over the edge and we are forced to use our wings to save ourselves from a fatal fall.

Look at your trials in this light, and see if you can't get a glimpse of their meaning, while your wings are being developed. There is no growth except in the fulfillment of obligations.

> Scripture: *"The Lord will keep you from all evil, he will keep your life*
>
> *The Lord will keep your going out and your coming in. From this time on and forevermore." Psalm 121: 7-8*

There is no fruit which is not bitter before it is ripe.

CHRISTMAS 2010
I CORINTHIAN 13, STYLE

If I decorated my house perfectly with plaid bows, strands of lights and shiny balls, but do not show love to my family, I'm just another **decorator.**

If I slave away in the kitchen baking dozens of cookies, preparing gourmet meals and arranging a beautifully adorned table at mealtime, but do not show love to my family, I'm just another **cook.**

If I work at the soup kitchen, carol in the nursing home and give all that I have to charity, but do not show love to my family, **it profits me nothing.**

If I trim the spruce with shimmering angels and crocheted snowflakes, attend a myriad of Holiday parties and sing in the church cantata but do not focus on **Christ,** I have missed the point

Love bears all things, believes all things, hopes all things, endures all things. Love never fails.

Giving the gift of Love will endure forever.

> "Love is patient, love is kind, love is not envious or boastful or arrogant or rude. It does not insist on its own way; it is not irritable or resentful; it is does not rejoice in wrongdoing, but rejoices in the truth. It bears all things, believes all things, hopes all things, and endures all things. Love never ends."
> 1 Cor. 13: 4-8

The best gifts to give this season, **with love,** are:

To a Friend . . . . Loyalty
To an Enemy . . . . Forgiveness
To the Boss . . . . Service

To your child . . . . A good example
To your Father . . . . Honor
To your Mother . . . . . . Gratitude and Devotion
To your Spouse . . . . Love and Faithfulness
To all Men . . . . Charity
To God . . . . Your Life!

Prayer

Symbols Of Christmas

Everyone has a favorite recipe that they like to use for Christmas. One may say that it is a **Symbol of Christmas.** Think for a moment about your favorite treat at Christmas. Maybe it is Plum Pudding, or Christmas Pie, or Red Velvet Praline Cake or Eggnog, or even a Christmas Roast Beef. Don't they **all** sound delicious? **Symbols of Christmas.**

In my family the Christmas Pie was the favorite. The girls clambered for the recipe. It was a pure white pie, in a pie shell that was made with a delicious cream filling containing bits of coconut, using vanilla and almond extract. It was just too good for anyone to ask how many calories it had. And every Christmas the girls would approach their mother asking for the recipe. Audrey would always gently refuse to give them her recipe, saying, "No, this is my special symbol of Christmas." So if you want the recipe you will have to come to see me at my **calling hour** and you will find it printed on the back of my memorial card. "Obviously, this did not set well with the girls who felt that their mom was being stingy and petty with her Christmas Pie desert.

Last Christmas, Audrey decided to share her guarded secret. We went to the shelf where the Betty Crocker Cook Book was kept . . . removed the page that the recipe was printed on and made exact copies for each of the girls. The page was tattered and worn, stained for having been used for so many Christmas' past. This was the cook book that the girls learned to cook with years before. How easy it is to over look the obvious. The oldest daughter was upset when she noticed that the grand-daughter had received the recipe in her envelope and without looking at her gift she proceeded to throw it down in disgust. After a few tears that quickly turned to smiles and then laughter the truth was revealed. What I want to share with you today is a recipe for **Christmas Joy.** Before I do, we need to define Christmas.

Here it is only days before Christmas and we are still making plans for the holidays. Perhaps we need to appreciate this time we call **Christmas.** Christmas is when we remember the anniversary of the birth of **Jesus**

Christ. Its observance is celebrated by most Protestants and Catholics on the **25ᵗʰ of December.** Eastern Orthodox churches celebrate Christmas on January 6ᵗʰ, the Armenian Churches on January 19ᵗʰ. The first mention of Christmas observances on December 25ᵗʰ was in the time of Constantine, about 325 AD.

The actual date of the birth of Christ in not known. The word **CHRISTMAS** is formed with two words, **Christ + Mass,** meaning a mass or religious service in commemoration of Jesus' birth.

And so we find ourselves preparing for a celebration of the **birth of God's Son.** In the Christian Church we have a period of seasons called Advent which prepares us for Christmas. These seasons are rich with traditions and symbols, many of which had their origin in pagan traditions. Christians turned many of these events into spiritual ways to help themselves, as well as new believers, to focus on **Jesus.**

Advent means "coming or arrival". Advent begins four weeks before Christmas and prepares for the celebration of the birth of Jesus the Christ and the anticipation of the return of **Christ the King** at his second coming. **The Advent Wreath** then becomes another symbol of Christmas.

Christmas Trees are another familiar symbol of Christmas. At this time of year when the leaves of the other trees have turned brown and fallen to the ground the evergreen tree keeps its fresh green look, encouraging us to be thankful for our lives. It is the symbol of **LIFE.**

At the beginning of the 19ᵗʰ century all of Germany had adopted the use of the green fir tree as the **Christmas Tree.** They would decorate the tree with candles and stars, hand-made ornaments, tiny toys and gilded nuts, so that all could enjoy the time of Jesus' birth.

The custom of the Christmas tree was brought to this country by the Pennsylvania Germans in 1820's. In 1923 President Calvin Coolidge directed the lighting of an outdoor tree at the White House., thereby starting a long standing tradition. President Obama lit the White House Tree this year decorated with more than 3,000 lights. To Christians the lighted tree with candles or electric bulbs, reminds us the **Jesus is the Light of the World, the light that we should follow.**

> *"I am the light for the world. Follow me, and you won't be walking in the dark.*
> *You will have the light that gives life."*
> *John 8:12*

There are many traditions and symbols for Christians. They include:

The Advent Wreath, The Bells of Christmas, Christmas Carols, Nativity Scenes, Poinsettia Plants, Fruit Cakes, Greeting cards, Mistletoe and Yule Logs, and so many more . . . .

But, I promised you a recipe for **Christmas Joy,** and here it is:

Ingredients:
1/2 cup of **hugs,** 4 teaspoons of **kisses,**
4 cups of **Love,** 1 cup of special Holiday **Cheer,**
3 Teaspoons of **Christian Spirits** 1/2 cup of **Peace on Earth**
2 cups of **Goodwill Towards Man**
1 sprig of **Mistletoe**
A medium sized bag of **Christmas Snowflakes.**

Preparation:
Mix hugs and kisses with Love until consistent. Blend in Holiday Cheer, Peace On Earth, Christmas Spirits and Good Will Towards Man.

Use the mixture to fill a large warm heart, where it can be stored for a life time. **It will never go bad.**

Serve as desired under mistletoe, sprinkle generously with Xmas Snowflakes.

This is especially good when accompanied by Christmas Carols at a family get together. **Serves One and All.**

Prayer

SPIRITUAL GIFTS

"I am the vine, you are the branches. Those who abide in me and I in them bear much fruit, because apart from me you can do nothing." (John 15:5)

God gives us abilities to glorify Him and to make disciples for Christ. These abilities are called **Spiritual Gifts.** We all have them, at least one or more, and we should be skilled in using them. They are given to us to be used in our ministry with Christ. They are for the purpose of bearing much fruit and exalting our Lord.

As the dish holding the M & Ms is passed take a candy and hold it in your hand. It is okay, they won't melt. Examine each candy carefully. Turn them over and around and you will see the **M** becomes a **W,** and then an **E** and finally the number **3.** They remind us of some of our **Spiritual Gifts.**

M is for **MERCY.** It reminds us to feel compassion for and take action in behalf of others in need.

W is for **WISDOM.** That we might bring spiritual insight or truth from a specific situation, to effectively meet a need or to solve a problem.

E is for **ENCOURAGEMENT.** So that we might strengthen, comfort or motivate people towards a deeper faith in Jesus Christ.

3 is a number. Which <u>always</u> represents the three in one, **FATHER, SON, AND HOLY SPIRIT.** The vine.

So as you eat these candies, or share them with your friends, remember the precious gift of Faith that we have in Jesus Christ and the spiritual gifts that are ours to use. We become the branches that bear much fruit.

Closing prayer

A Story Of Wealth—Love And Success

People come into our lives for a **Reason**, a **Season** or a **Lifetime**. When you know which one it is, you will know what to do for that person. When someone is in your life for a **Reason,** it is usually to meet a need you have expressed. They have come to assist you through a difficultly, to provide you with guidance and support, or to aid you physically, emotionally or spiritually.

They may seem like a Godsend, and they are . . . They are there for the **reason** you need them. And we certainly thank God for providing that help.

Then, without any wrongdoing on your part or at an inconvenient time, that person may say something, or do something to bring the relationship to an end. Sometimes they die. Sometimes they walk away. Sometimes they act up and force you to take a stand. What we must realize is that our need has been met. Out desire fulfilled and their work is done.

The prayer that you asked God for has been answered and now it is time to move on.

Some people come into your life for a **Season,** because your time has come to share and grow or learn. They bring you an experience of peace or make you laugh. They teach you something you have never done before. They usually give you an unbelievable amount of joy. Believe it . . . . it is real. But only for a season.

Lifetime relationships teach you lifetime lessons, Things that you will build on in order to have a solid emotional foundation. Your job is to accept the lesson. Love the person and put what you have learned to use. Use them in all other relationships and areas of your life. **It is said that love is blind but friendship is clairvoyant.**

Ephesians 5:15-16 says: *"So be careful how you live, not as fools but as those who are wise. Make the most of every opportunity for doing good in these evil days."*

A story:

A woman came out of her house one morning and saw three old men with long white beards sitting in the front yard. She didn't recognize them so she approached them and said, "I don't know you, but you must be hungry or thirsty. Would you like to come in and have something to eat?"

"Is the man of the house at home?" asked one of the men. No! She replied: "He is at work".

"Then we cannot come in." they said.

In the evening when her husband returned, she told him what had happened. "Go tell them I am at home and invite them to join us," he said. So the woman went out to speak to the old men.

"We don't go into a house together," was the answer. "Why is that?" asked the woman One of the men explained that his name is **Wealth**, and pointing his finger at his friends he said this is **Success** and the other man's name is **Love.** Then he added, "Please go in and discuss this with your husband." Ask him which one of us do you want in your home?"

The woman went into the house and told her husband what had happened. Her husband was overjoyed. He said, "'If this is the case let's invite **Wealth.**" Let him come in and fill our home with wealth. We can have everything that we want.

His wife disagreed. "My dear, why don't we invite **Success**?" Then we will always be successful. "Wait a minute", said their daughter, who had been listening quietly in the back room. "Wouldn't it be better to invite **Love.**" "Our home would then be filled with love."

"Let us heed our daughter's advice," said the husband. "Go out and invite **Love** to be our guest."

The woman went out and asked the three old men, "Which one of you is **Love**?" Please come in and join us. **Love** got up and started to walk toward the house, but the other two men also got up and followed him. Surprised, the woman asked **Wealth** and **Success,** "Where are you going? Why are you coming as well?"

The old men replied in unison, "If you had invited either **Wealth** or **Success** the other two of us would have had to stay out. But since you invited **Love**, wherever love goes, we go with him." ***Where there is Love there is also Wealth and Success.***

My Wish for You

Where there is pain, I wish you peace and mercy.

Where there is self-doubt, I wish you renewed confidence and the ability to work it out.

Where there is tiredness, or exhaustion, I wish you understanding, patience and renewed strength.

Where there is fear, I wish you love and courage.

Remember, the best sermons are lived, not preached.

Closing prayer

A SMALL GESTURE MAY MAKE
A BLESSING

Many people pass through our lives but only **real friends** leave their imprint on our hearts.

Last Saturday, your worship team was honored at a banquet by ABCORI (American Baptist Churches of Rhode Island) for the contributions to shut-ins and folks in nursing homes in Rhode Island. Mary Ostiguy and Ginny Mancini have been faithful in coming to Roberts Health Center for many years. Mary has been active for nearly 40 years. I am proud to be a member of their team and we have been blessed with the opportunity to serve.

Our scripture reading is found in Psalm 100: 5 and we read of how David sings about praising God. *"For the Lord is good: His steadfast love endures forever, and he is faithful to all generations."*

An act of goodness that is done today can come back to you, or someone you love, when you least expect it. And so it is! As the honor given by ABCORI this week. I would like to share a story about how a seemingly small gesture certainly became a blessing.

One day a poor boy was going door to door selling home goods and cleaning supplies. He was working to pay for his education. As he went along knocking on doors and talking with home owners he became very hungry and he only had 10 cents in his pocket. So, he decided he should ask someone for something to eat.

The next house that he came to was a beautiful Victorian house. It was big, and it was well maintained. It had man flower and shrubs around it. Certainly someone with money must live there. As he approached the front door and rang the door bell a young woman greeted him with a friendly hello and a big smile. The boy forgot about being hungry but he asked the girl if he could have a drink of water.

The girl thought the boy looked very hungry so instead of water she brought him a large glass of milk. He drank the milk very slowly, savoring very drop. When he finished he asked, "How much do I owe You?" You don't owe me anything, she replied, "My mother taught me never to accept anything for doing something kind for someone in need."

He replied, "Then I thank you from the bottom of my heard." When Howard Kelly left the house he was refreshed. He had a feeling of physical strength and he sensed a return of his faith in the Lord. He had been so busy working to earn money for school he had nearly abandoned his faith.

Years later, the same young girl fell gravely ill. Te local doctors were mystified by her illness so they recommended that she be taken to the big city where they knew she could see a specialist who might be able to diagnose the rare disease and possibly help her.

Doctor Howard Kelly was called as a consultant. When he heard the name of the town in which the patient lived, it triggered his memory of an event that he had had years before. He went directly to the woman's room and quickly recognized her. He returned to his office and promised that he would do the very best that he could do to save her life. From that day on he saw her very day and paid special attention to her progress. After a long battle the woman recovered.

Doctor Kelly left instructi9ns that the bill for this woman's care should be sent to him for his review. When it arrived he looked it over, wrote something in the margin and put it in an envelope, sealed it and instructed his staff to leave it in the woman's room.

The woman thought that when she opened the mail that she would find an invoice that would take the rest of her life to pay-in-full. But when she read the bill something caught her attention: In the margin of the invoice she read these words: **"Paid in Full with a glass of milk."** signed, Howard Kelly, MD

Tears of joy filled her eyes and touched her heart. She prayed, **"Thank you Lord for your love which has crossed the hands and the heart of man."**

If you receive a blessing, pass it on. A blessing cannot be kept. If it stops with the recipient the blessing disappears. If we receive a blessing we need to keep it working by being the source of the blessing to other people.

The hardest lesson in life is to know which bridges to cross and which to burn.

Prayer.

Rules To Live By

As we travel life's journey we find that there many rules that we need to follow. Many think that the rules have been made for the other guy and it isn't necessary to follow them. Some think that they can pick and choose the rules and blame someone else for making them. The politically correct expression is, **"I have my rights."** Some believe they can make up the rules and do as they please. But, we all know that is not the case.

Psalm 66:7 speaks of God and says, *"He rules forever by His power, His eyes watch the nations—let not the rebellious rise up against him"*.

How many of you remember the old clothes lines? Even hanging clothes on the clothesline had a set of rules. **Remember: W**hen you hung up socks you hung them by the toe and not the top? And, you never hung pants by the waistband, always by the cuff or bottom.

There were **10** commandments or rules when hanging clothes on the line:

1. It was necessary to wash the clothes-line before hanging any clothes. You walked the entire length of each line with a damp cloth to be certain they were clean.
2. You had to hang the clothes in a certain order. Always hang the whites with the whites and always hang them first.
3. You never hung the shirt by the shoulders—always by the tail. (What would the neighbors think?)
4. Wash Day was Monday. Never hang clothes on Sunday or on the weekend. (Caution the Blue Laws.)
5. Hang the sheets and the towels on the outside lines so that you could hide your unmentionables in the middle. (Think of the perverts and busybodies, passing by.)
6. Zero weather? Didn't matter, the clothes would **"freeze-dry"**

7. If you were efficient you would lineup the clothes so that each item did not need two clothes pins. Share each pin with the next washed item.

8. Remove the clothes from the clothes-line before dinner. Neatly fold the clothes in the clothes basket so they will be ready to be **ironed.**

9. Always gather the clothes pins when taking down the dry clothes. Pins left on the lines are tacky

10. **IRONED!** Well, that is a whole different subject. (Forget the wash and wear fabrics.)

A poem: **Ode To A Clothesline**

A clothesline was a news forecast.
To neighbors passing by.
There were no secrets you could keep,
When clothes hung out to dry.

It also had a friendly link
For neighbors always knew,
If company had stopped in
To spend a night or two.

For then you see the *fancy sheets,*
And *towels* on the line,
You'd see the company *table clothes*
With intricate design.

The line announced a baby's birth
Of folks who lived inside-
As brand-new infant clothes were hung
So carefully with pride.

The ages of the children
Could readily be known.
By watching how the sizes changed
You'd know how much they had grown.

It also told when illness struck
As extra sheets were hung.
Then nightclothes, and a bathrobe, too
Haphazardly were strung.

It also said, "Gone On Vacation"
When the lines were limp and bare,
It told "We're Back!' when lines sagged
With not a inch to spare.

New folks in town were scorned upon
If the wash was dingy-gray
As neighbors carefully raised their brows
And looked the other way.

But clothes lines now are of the past
For dryers make work much less
Now what goes on inside the home
Is anybody's guess.

I really miss that way of life
It had a friendly sign
When neighbors knew each other best
By what hung on the line

As a postscript I must say there is nothing better than sleeping on fresh sheets that have been hanging on the line. AND SO IT IS.

FLYING LOOKING UP

There are many interesting facts and trivia about flying. It has been a little more that 100 years ago that the Wright Brothers flew the first fixed wing airplane. One has to be amazed at the advances in technology that have evolved from the first flight at Kitty Hawk, NC., where Orville and Wilbur Wright flew their first airplane a distance of less than the wing span of a modern Boeing 747 jet airliner.

Now we have a new large A-380 Air Bus that is powered by four Rolls-Royce Trent engines that develop 70,000 pounds of thrust each. They propel the airplane that weighs **one-million 250,000 pounds** to an altitude of more than 41,000 feet at a speed of .87 Mach or 600 mph.

The airplane can carry 823 passengers, to a distance of 9400 miles with all of the comforts and amenities known to mankind. The runway requirements for takeoff at sea level for the A-380 Air Bus is 9,023 feet, or nearly two miles in length.

A Gates Learjet LR-35 corporate jet carrying 8 to 10 passengers can fly a distance of 2000 miles at 600 mph and it has a takeoff requirement of 5,300 feet. A reasonably long runway requirement for a small jet.

And, a S-76 Sikorsky helicopter can fly 6 passengers from a standing position, to another heliport or airport a distance of 300 miles away at 250 knots with no runway required at all.

And so it is with aviation.

However, do you know if you put a **buzzard** in a pen that is 6 feet by 8 feet and is entirely open at the top the bird, in spite of its ability to fly, it will not take off. The reason is the buzzard always begins a flight from the ground with a run of 10 to 12 feet. Without space for it to run it is like the Air Bus on a 5000 foot runway. It will not attempt to fly. It will remain a prisoner for life in a small enclosure with no top.

An ordinary **Bat** flies around at night and is a remarkably nimble creature in the air. But a bat cannot take off from a level place. If it is placed on the floor or on some flat ground all it will do is shuffle around helplessly with pain, until it reaches some slight elevation from which it can throw itself into the air. When that happens it takes off like a flash. Or, "A Bat out of Hell!"

A **Bumblebee** if dropped into an open glass tumbler will be there until it dies, unless it is taken out. It never sees the means of escape at the top but persists in trying to find some way out through the sides near the bottom. It will seek a way where none exists, until it destroys itself.

People in many ways are like the buzzard, the bat, and the bumblebee. They struggle with their problems and frustrations never realizing that all they have to do is **look up.**

Therein lies the answer. The answer, the escape route, the solution to any problem is to simply **look up.**

Sorrow looks back. Worry looks around, but Faith looks up.

> **". . . you seek the Lord your God and you will find him if you look for him with all your heart and all your soul when you are in distress and things happen to you, then in the later days you will return to the Lord your God nd obey him. For the Lord your God is a merciful God, he will not abandon or destroy you or forget the covenant with your forefathers, which he confirmed to them by oath."**
> Deuteronomy 4:290-30.

LIVE SIMPLY
LOVE GENEROUSLY
CARE DEEPLY
SPEAK KINDLY
AND TRUST IN GOD WHO LOVES YOU.

"Those who **look** to Him are radiant, their faces are never covered with shame."
Psalm 34:

Prayer

FLY AGAIN

Words and music by David Phelps

His trembling hands held the church pew that day,
Struggling to stand when they asked him to pray.
With wisdom and strength his words were spoken
But his body grew weary for his wings were broken.
But he will fly once again.

He will soar with his wings unfolded;
Hear the angels applaud
As he rides on the wind, to the arms of God.
And he will fly. He will fly again.

And on that day when he left for the sky,
I saw him smile as he told me goodbye.
No more would he weep for missed tomorrows,
No more would he suffer in this land of sorrows.
But he will fly once again.

He will soar with his wings unfolded.
Hear the angels applaud
As he rides on the wind to the arms of God.
And he will fly. He will fly again.

I know that he's in a better place.
I still dream of the day when I'll see his face.v
Then we'll embrace, and never to end
We will fly once again.

We will soar with our wings unfolded
Hear the angels applaud.
As we ride on the wind to the arms of God.
And we will fly. We will fly again.

THE NEED TO FLY

I watch as he turns to leave the hangar.
His eyes scroll about as he takes it all in.
My heart feels the ties I know he is breaking.
I see a blink, then a tear, as he tries to grin.

Weather, flight plans, near and far destinations.
That's how he has lived this gentleman.
This decision, put off for so long,
Says let's "wrap it up" that is the plan.

The love for all he is, hits me so hard,
Watching his face like a living cue card.
The list of his losses he alone must review,
Will he allow me to help him get through?

Thousands of miles across the great sky.
Loving the privilege of his own wings to fly.
Seeing the world from a lofty view,
While modestly saying "well that's what I do."

A surprise in the offing is what we both need.
Time for the grandkids, and each other indeed.
Homebodies on outings by car or by air
It won't matter to me as long as he's there.

Leisurely outings not controlled by a clock.
A hand-holding stroll down to some dock.
Time to give back for all that has been,
Making room for each other away from life's din.

A prayer by Jabez was the very first glue.
Each was alone, but life's better by two,

195

This time in life may we spend it together.
This our own Autumn, life's sweetest weather.

Thank God for the blessings of this . . . our love.

Audrey C. Schmid